GRAND CANYON NATIONAL PARK

★★★★★★★★★★★★★★★★★★★★★★★★★★★★★★★★★★★★★★

Edited by ROBERT SCHARFF
with the cooperation of the
NATIONAL PARK SERVICE

★★★★★★★★★★★★★★★★★★★★★★★★★★★★★★★★★★★★★★

DAVID McKAY COMPANY, INC.
NEW YORK

GRAND CANYON NATIONAL PARK

COPYRIGHT © 1967 BY ROBERT SCHARFF

LIBRARY OF CONGRESS CATALOG CARD NUMBER: 67-13550

MANUFACTURED IN THE UNITED STATES OF AMERICA

foreword

THE Grand Canyon is so many things.

First, for all its vastness, it is a vise: It grips you, takes hold of your emotions.

Then, it is wings: It carries you aloft, permits your spirit to soar.

Now, it seems a prism, taking the light of sunrise or sunset, breaking it up into ever-changing patterns . . . waves of color that wash against the awesome mile-high cliffs and clefts.

The first time I saw the Canyon, I was ten years old. Since then, I have seen it often, but never with less surprise or amazement than the time before. For the Canyon is an experience that grows . . . with you.

I have walked the rim and looked down the deep toward the Colorado River, still gouging the rock as it has for millions of years. And I have lived on that river, too, and for days, riding the calm water, riding the water whipped into rapids. Then, looking up from a sand bar respite in the downstream journey, I have been overcome, not by fatigue, but by the exhilaration that comes from living even briefly with the grandeur and overwhelming power of this greatest of nature's carvings on earth.

The Grand Canyon makes you want to shake your head, now and then, as though to clear away the webs of uncertainty. You want to ask yourself whether it is so, whether such things exist, are real.

Yes, the Canyon is real . . . as real and as limitless as your own capacity to wonder and to dream, and for that, it is a key of sorts, too . . . a key to you!

Try it!

It is yours!

STEWART L. UDALL
Secretary of the Interior

acknowledgments

To put a book like this together requires a great deal of help. And I certainly received it from the National Park Service and the concessioners at Grand Canyon National Park. Chief Naturalist Merrill D. Beal and his assistant, James W. Schaack, helped greatly in the gathering of material and checked both the manuscript and proofs for accuracy. In addition, I would like to thank Superintendent Howard B. Stricklin and other members of his staff including Stanley T. Albright, Theodore R. Thompson, Vernon Ruesch, and Louise M. Hinchliffe. I am indebted to the Grand Canyon Natural History Association for use of certain material from their publications. I would also like to thank Superintendent John F. Turney of Walnut Canyon National Monument and Archaeologist George J. Chambers of Wupatki-Sunset Crater National Monuments for their assistance with material for Chapter 7.

Among the concessioners, Joseph Ernst, Tom Menaugh, Troy LeGrand, John M. Cunningham, Evelyn Lukkonen, Jay Goza, and Robert W. Pothier of the Fred Harvey organization, T. E. Murray of the Utah Parks Company, and Richard V. Herre of Union Pacific Railroad Company have been especially helpful in the preparation of the book. The photographs used in this book are by courtesy of the National Park Service, Fred Harvey, Union Pacific Railroad Company, and Santa Fe Railroad Company.

ROBERT SCHARFF

Contents

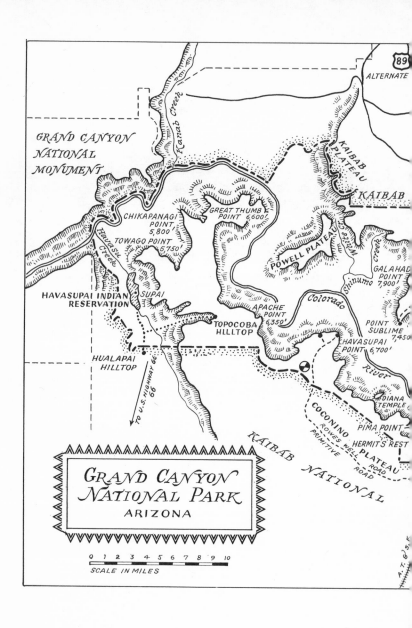

GRAND CANYON NATIONAL MONUMENT

U.S. 89 ALTERNATE

KAIBAB PLATEAU

KAIBAB

Kanab Creek

CHIKAPANAGI POINT, 5,800

GREAT THUMB POINT 6,600'

POWELL PLATEAU

Shinumo Creek

GALAHAD POINT 7,900'

TOWAGO POINT 5,750'

Havasu Creek

SUPAI

HAVASUPAI INDIAN RESERVATION

APACHE POINT 6,350'

Colorado

POINT SUBLIME 7,450

TOPOCOBA HILLTOP

HAVASUPAI POINT 6,700'

HUALAPAI HILLTOP

TO U.S. HIGHWAY 66

River

DIANA TEMPLE

PIMA POINT

COCONINO
ROWES WELL
PRIMITIVE
ROAD

HERMIT'S REST

KAIBAB NATIONAL

PLATEAU

GRAND CANYON
NATIONAL PARK
ARIZONA

0 1 2 3 4 5 6 7 8 9 10
SCALE IN MILES

A.T.&S.F.

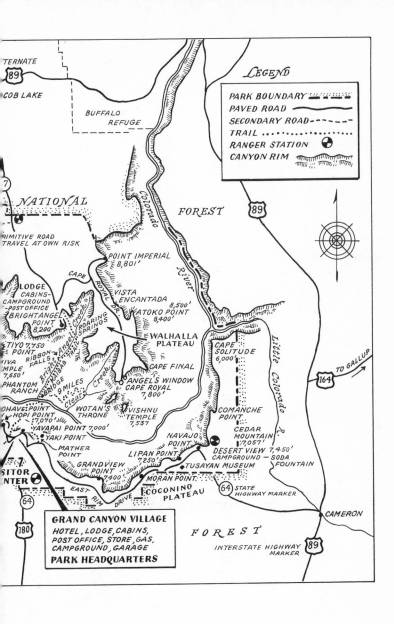

TERNATE
89
COB LAKE

BUFFALO REFUGE

NATIONAL

FOREST

89

PRIMITIVE ROAD
TRAVEL AT OWN RISK

POINT IMPERIAL
8,801'

Colorado

River

CAPE

ROYAL DR.

LODGE
CABINS-
CAMPGROUND
-POST OFFICE
BRIGHTANGEL
POINT
8,200'

VISTA
ENCANTADA
8,500'
ATOKO POINT
8,400'

ROARING
SPRINGS

TIYO 7,750
POINT

RIBBON
FALLS

WALHALLA
PLATEAU

Bright Angel Creek

Kaibab Trail

IVA
MPLE
7,650'

BRIDGE

9 MILES

CAPE FINAL

PHANTOM
RANCH

Clear
Creek

ANGEL'S WINDOW
CAPE ROYAL
7,800'

CAPE
SOLITUDE
6,000'

Little Colorado R.

TO GALLUP

164

OHAVE POINT
HOPI POINT
7,070'
YAVAPAI POINT 7,000'
YAKI POINT

WOTAN'S
THRONE

VISHNU
TEMPLE
7,537

COMANCHE
POINT

MATHER
Point

NAVAJO
POINT

CEDAR
MOUNTAIN
7,057'

7

SITOR
NTER

GRANDVIEW
POINT
7,400'

LIPAN POINT
7,250'

DESERT VIEW 7,450'
CAMPGROUND — SODA
FOUNTAIN

TUSAYAN MUSEUM

MORAN POINT

64

EAST
RIM
DRIVE

COCONINO
PLATEAU

64
180

STATE
HIGHWAY MARKER

CAMERON

GRAND CANYON VILLAGE
HOTEL, LODGE, CABINS,
POST OFFICE, STORE, GAS,
CAMPGROUND, GARAGE
PARK HEADQUARTERS

FOREST

INTERSTATE HIGHWAY
MARKER

89

Chapter 1.

The Grandeur of Grand Canyon

THE Grand Canyon is a gigantic rock-walled chasm four to eighteen miles wide, deeply incised at both Rims, and at the Inner Gorge, which walls the present stream bed of the Colorado River. There are numerous side canyons and an intermediate plateau area known as the Tonto, which is approximately 3,500 to 3,700 feet lower in elevation than the South Rim. The Canyon separates the Coconino Plateau on the south from the Kaibab Plateau on the north. Grand Canyon Village on the South Rim is at an elevation of approximately 7,000 feet above sea level. The North Rim at Grand Canyon Lodge is approximately 8,200 feet elevation. In striking contrast, Phantom Ranch, near the juncture of the Bright Angel Creek with the Colorado River at the bottom of the Canyon, is 2,550 feet in elevation.

While only a very few topographical features in the Park have been designated as "mountains"—Cedar Mountain, Mount Hayden, Saddle Mountain—numberless buttes and mesas within the Canyon are in reality recessed mountains. Although these features are looked down upon from the Rims, several of them are higher than the highest mountains in the eastern United States.

As first glimpsed from the very edge of the abyss, the Canyon is a geologic marvel and invokes spiritual emotion. Below is a primeval void, hemmed in everywhere except skyward, by the solid framework of our earth—rocks and rocks, and yet more rocks, millions of years old.

From hour to hour the colors of the Grand Canyon change, responding to the direction of sunlight and to atmospheric conditions. This view is from El Tovar Point near Grand Canyon Village. Fred Harvey photo.

At high noon the enclosing walls seem to flatten out and are unimpressive. They lack life and luster and form. They make scant appeal to the emotions. One is aware of bigness and deepness and stillness, but not of any mystery.

Come back to the edge of the abyss in the late afternoon or early in the morning. How marvelous the transformation! Immense forms have pushed out from the sheer walls. They float in a purple sea of mysterious shadows. It is a symphony of mass and color, of body and soul. Almost a new heaven is born, and with it a new inferno, swathed in soft celestial fires; a whole chaotic underworld just emptied of primeval floods and waiting for a new creative word; eluding all sense of perspective of dimension, outstretching the faculty of measurement, overlapping the confines of definite apprehension; a boding, terrible thing, unflinchingly real, yet spectral as a dream. Never was picture more harmonious, never flower more exquisitely beautiful. It flashes instant communication of everything that architecture and painting and music for a thousand years have striven to express.

Should it chance to have rained heavily in the night, next morning the Canyon may be completely filled with fog. As the sun mounts, the curtain of mist suddenly breaks into cloud fleeces, and while you gaze, these fleeces rise and dissipate, leaving the Canyon bare. At once around the bases of the lowest cliffs white puffs begin to appear and their number multiplies until once more they rise and overflow the rim, and it is as if you stood on some land's end looking down upon a formless void. Then quickly comes the complete dissipation, and again the marshaling in the depths, the upward advance, the total suffusion and the speedy vanishing, repeated over and over until the warm walls have expelled their saturation. It is, indeed, a place created by some magician's wand.

Long may the visitor loiter upon the verge, powerless to shake loose from the charm, until the sun is low in the West. Then the Canyon sinks into mysterious purple shadow, the far Shinumo Altar is tipped with a golden ray, and against a leaden horizon the long line of the Echo Cliffs reflects a soft brilliance of indescribable beauty, a light that, elsewhere, surely never was on sea or land. Then darkness falls, and should there be a moon, the scene in part revives in silver light a thousand spectral forms projected from inscrutable gloom; dreams of mountains, as in their sleep they brood on things eternal.

The Grand Canyon of Arizona is beyond comprehension. It is the sum total of all the aspects of nature combined in one integrated whole. It is at once the smile and the frown upon the face of Nature. In its heart is the savage, uncontrollable fury of all the inanimate universe, and at the same time the immeasurable serenity that succeeds it. But always, in whatever mood, it grips and humbles and uplifts—for here is the ultimate in beauty and grandeur.

MAN AND THE GRAND CANYON

The walls of the Grand Canyon and the plateaus along both its Rims hold the story of the prehistoric people who lived there. While archeological evidence indicates that early man lived in the Southwest twenty-eight thousand years ago, the earliest known discoveries in the Park itself, are split-twig figurines found in dry caves. They have been dated by radioactive carbon methods at three thousand years old. These were presumably fetishes made by primitive people who were hunters and gatherers of the natural harvest of the land. Not much else is known about them.

The Basket Makers appeared in the Southwest over two thousand years ago. (As implied by the name, the Basket Makers made excellent baskets.) They lived in caves and primitive pit homes. A few pit-house ruins and other sites have been discovered in the Canyon. A group similar to the Basket Makers called the Cohonina occupied the South Rim one thousand four hundred years ago as indicated by a site near Desert View. The first Pueblo people appeared in the region about one thousand two hundred years ago. (The word "pueblo" is a Spanish word meaning "village," and is applied to these people, and to the large but closely built villages that they learned to construct.) Several ruins and many archeological sites from this period are found in the Park, especially on the Walhalla Plateau (North Rim) and near the Tusayan Ruin at Desert View on the South Rim. The Havasupai Indians, who moved into the Canyon probably in the 1400's, still make their home in Havasu Canyon, the *only* Indian reservation found within the boundaries of a National Park.

In 1540 Europeans saw the Grand Canyon for the first time. In that year, Francisco Vásques Coronado, the Spanish governor of Galacia, left Mexico with an army of several hundred in search of the "Seven Cities of Cibola," an Indian kingdom rumored to be fabulously rich in gold. While Coronado and his men found no gold, they did discover what is now New Mexico and Arizona. Don Pedro

3

de Tovar led a detachment of Conquistadores that explored the province of Tusayan, the area now known as the land of the Hopis. While among the Hopi Indians, Tovar heard tales of "a great river and chasm" lying to the west and reported them to Coronado.

To verify the story, Coronado sent Captain Garcia Lopez de Cardenas and twelve other soldiers to investigate. After twenty days of difficult travel, they came upon the South Rim of the great chasm. Several of the Conquistadores made an unsuccessful effort to reach the river below but found "the buttes and towers, that appeared from above to be the height of a man, were higher than the tower of the Cathedral of Seville."

No further mention of the Canyon area is made until 1776 when it was visited independently by two Spanish priests, Father Garces and Father Escalante. In the detailed diary of his trip across Northern Arizona and Havasupai Indian country, Father Garces described the region and is often credited with naming the river, "Colorado." (Colorado means "red" in Spanish and it is not hard to understand why this tawny torrent was called the "red river.") While Father Escalante did not visit the Grand Canyon itself, as far as we know, he spanned the river at the Old Ute Ford near the head of Glen Canyon; henceforth this location has been called "El Vado de los Padres"—The Crossing of the Fathers.

For more than eighty years thereafter the Canyon remained unvisited except by Indians, a few Mormon herdsmen, and some trappers, although the Captain Lorenzo Sitgreaves expedition of 1851, journeying westward, struck the river about 150 miles above Yuma, and Lieutenant Amiel W. Whipple in 1854 made a survey for a practicable railroad route along the thirty-fifth parallel, where a railroad afterwards was constructed.

In 1857 the War Department dispatched an expedition in charge of Lieutenant Joseph Christmas Ives to explore the Colorado upstream to the head of navigation. Ives ascended to the head of Black Canyon; then returning to the Needles, he set off northeast across

---

Grand Canyon's immensity has allowed it to swallow its own cloud-capped mountain range. Visitors look down on these captive peaks from Bright Angel Point on the Canyon's North Rim. This view of Deva, Brahma, and Zoroaster Temples, and Bright Angel Canyon was once used on a 2¢ stamp. Union Pacific Railroad photo.

country. He reached the Canyon at Diamond and Havasu Creeks in the spring of 1858, and made a wide southward detour around the neighboring San Francisco mountain peaks, thence to the Hopi pueblos, to Fort Defiance, and back to civilization.

"Ours has been the first, and will doubtless be the last, party of whites to visit this profitless locality," reported Lieutenant Ives, after vainly trying to reach the Rim of the Canyon. There is perhaps more poetry than prophecy in his later statement: "It seems intended by nature that the Colorado River, along the greater part of its lonely and majestic way, shall be forever unvisited and undisturbed."

It remained for a geologist and a schoolteacher, a one-armed veteran of the Civil War, John Wesley Powell, afterward Director of the United States Geological Survey, to dare and to accomplish the exploration of the mighty river.

In 1869 Major Powell started with nine men and four boats from Green River City, on the Green River, in Wyoming. The project met with the most urgent remonstrance from those who were best acquainted with the region, including the Indians, who maintained that boats could not possibly live in any one of a score of rapids and falls known to them, to say nothing of the vast unknown stretches in which at any moment a Niagara might be disclosed. It was also then believed that for hundreds of miles the river disappeared wholly beneath the surface of the earth. Powell launched his flotilla on May 24, and on August 30 landed at the mouth of the Virgin River, more than one thousand miles by the river channel from the place of starting, minus two boats and four men. One of the men had left the expedition by way of an Indian reservation agency before reaching Arizona, and three, after holding out against unprecedented terrors for many weeks, had finally become daunted, choosing to encounter the perils of an unknown desert rather than to brave any longer the frightful menaces of that Stygian torrent. These three, unfortunately making their appearance on the plateau at a time when a recent depredation was colorably chargeable upon them, were killed by Indians, their story of having come thus far down the river in boats being wholly discredited by their captors.

Powell's journal of the trip is a fascinating tale, written in a compact and modest style, which, in spite of its reticence, tells an epic story of purest heroism. It definitely established the scene of his exploration as the most wonderful geological and spectacular phenomenon known to mankind, and justified the name which had been

6

bestowed upon it—*The Grand Canyon*. But, he did not abandon his exploration after the first dangerous and difficult trip.

Again, in 1871, Major Powell started down river with three boats and went as far as the Crossing of the Fathers. In the summer of 1872 he returned to the boats at Lee's Ferry, and descended through the Grand Canyon and went as far as the mouth of Kanab Wash, where the river journey was abandoned.

Since Powell's time, thousands of people have descended the Colorado River, some to survey, to study geology, botany, to photograph, and some simply for adventure. (You may see one of these journeys re-created in the motion pictures taken by Emery and Ellsworth Kolb in 1911. These films are shown every day on the South Rim at the Kolb Studio.) Some travelers of the Colorado have used rowboats, speedboats, outboard motorboats, and some rubber life rafts. (A fine collection of many of the boats that have made the river journey can be found in the courtyard of the Visitor Center on the South Rim.) Despite these sallies down the river and trips along the Rims, the tributary canyons, amphitheaters, and the Outer Canyon are rarely visited.

Tourist travel to the Canyon began in the 1880's thanks to the efforts of Captain John Hance. He first visited the area in 1883 while on a prospecting tour, and stayed until his death in 1919. On his homestead, approximately fifteen miles east of the Visitor Center and Park Headquarters, Hance erected the first building on the South Rim, a log cabin at the head of his trail leading to his copper and asbestos claims. Hance's trail was the first privately built route into the colorful gorge and down its narrow path the early tourists were to enjoy the full magnitude and depth of the Canyon.

When visitors began to arrive, Hance welcomed them to his homestead where they pitched their tents around his cabin. In 1886 he advertised himself in the Flagstaff newspaper, *The Arizona Champion,* as a guide to tourists, and though his accommodations were rough and limited, countless persons responded. They were drawn by a newly awakened interest in the Canyon, by Hance's congeniality as a host, and by his widening fame as a storyteller. As more visitors arrived each year, Hance erected another log building to serve as a dining hall and kitchen. Scattered under the pines within a stone's throw of the Rim was a tent city, with small tents for ladies and a large dormitory-type tent for the men. Travelers knew none of the superb accommodations people find today, but did share with equal

7

rapture the splendor of the Canyon spread out before them. In the years that followed several hotels were built, including the Grandview Hotel (1892), El Tovar (1904), Phantom Ranch (1921), the Grand Canyon Lodge (1928), and Bright Angel Lodge (1934). Several other tourist enterprises were started; Kolb Brothers Studio in 1903, Babbitt Brothers Store in 1905, Fred Harvey in 1904, and Verkamp's Store in 1906. The Santa Fe Railway completed its tracks to the South Rim in 1901; the first automobile arrived at the Park in 1902.

From 1885 until about 1910 over a hundred mining ventures were started in the Canyon. Only a few were profitable. Most were copper mines like the Bass Mine, Last Chance Mine and Daniel Hogan's mine, which later became the Orphan Uranium Mine which is located near Hopi Point. A little lead and asbestos were also mined, but due to transportation and other problems, proved not to be of economic value. (Mining is prohibited in the Park except on privately owned land, such as is the case of the Orphan Mine on the South Rim which is producing uranium.) Many of the trails were built during the early mining period and are still visible—some are still usable—even today. But very few historical buildings are still standing. The Hance Cabin, Grandview Hotel, and a few other old structures were razed before the Park Service acquired the property.

The movement to protect the Canyon began in 1886, when Senator Benjamin Harrison, of Indiana, introduced a bill to make it a National Park. Opposition by both public and private interests delayed the passage of such a bill for more than thirty years. In 1893, as President of the United States, Harrison established the Grand Canyon Forest Preserve; but the area was still open to exploitation by mining and lumbering interests.

President Theodore Roosevelt, after his first trip to the Canyon in 1903, said, "Do nothing to mar its grandeur . . . keep it for your children, your children's children, and all who come after you, as the one great sight which every American should see." In 1908, he established Grand Canyon National Monument. (National Monuments are set aside to preserve parts of our country containing historic, prehistoric, and scientific objects and features. Monuments are established by act of Congress or by Presidential proclamation, while National Parks require legislation to be introduced in Congress and then be approved by the President.) Finally, an act of Congress signed on February 26, 1919 by President Wilson established Grand

8

Canyon National Park—the first to be discovered—as the seventeenth member of the National Park System.

Today, the Grand Canyon National Park encompasses both the North and South Rims and covers 673,575 acres or 1,052 square miles. The actual length of the Park is 56 miles, yet the Colorado River winds its way for some 106 miles within the Park boundaries.

The eastern boundary of the Park includes the lofty colorful walls of the Canyon beyond which lies the Painted Desert, and runs along the east base of Cedar Mountain, the flat-topped butte which may be seen two or three miles to the east of Desert View. Its northern and southern boundary is the Kaibab National Forest, while its western boundaries include the watershed of the beautiful Havasu Canyon and the Grand Canyon National Monument. The latter is a primitive area about 310 square miles (198,280 acres) of land established in 1932 by Presidential proclamation. The major portion of the Monument lies north of the Colorado River between Kanab Creek on the east and the Pine Mountains and Lake Mead National Recreation Area on the west, embracing approximately 40 miles of the Grand Canyon. The highest peak, named Mount Trumbull by Major Powell (for Senator Lyman Trumbull of Connecticut) has an elevation of 8,028 feet above sea level. At Toroweap Point one of the most impressive views in the Canyon awaits you. Looking straight down the sheer rock walls, you can see the snakelike Colorado River, 3,000 feet below. Such a view is not possible in the National Park.

ADMINISTRATION OF THE PARK

Grand Canyon National Park is administered by the National Park Service, United States Department of the Interior. Affairs within the Park are directed by a superintendent, assisted by personnel trained in the fields of protection, interpretation, maintenance, and administration, and their duties include most of the operations ordinarily performed by state, county, and local governments.

The superintendent in the Park is personally responsible for the establishment of broad policies and for the success of overall management, including maintenance of satisfactory public-service standards by private concessioners operating within the Park. This is done within National Park Service guidelines, and with the assistance of National Park Service staff specialists when necessary. The super-

9

intendent is assisted by an assistant superintendent. While there are four major divisions in the Park operations—administration, maintenance, ranger services, and interpretation—the latter two are the ones a visitor usually meets. The superintendent of Grand Canyon National Park, whose address is Grand Canyon, Arizona 86023, is in immediate charge of Grand Canyon National Monument, too.

PARK RANGERS

Uniformed Park Rangers are responsible for enforcement of rules and regulations in the Park, fire detection and suppression, operation of entrance stations, and general supervision of activities in several districts into which the Park is divided. They also handle lost and found property and receive suggestions and complaints from visitors.

If you are in any sort of difficulty or need information, see a Park Ranger. He is there to help you. You will find them at Entrance Stations, Ranger Stations, and patrolling roads and campgrounds. Remember, however, that he is also a Park police officer, commanding the same respect you give such an officer at home. He is authorized to issue summons for the violator of a Park regulation to appear before the U.S. Commissioner at Park Headquarters. Persons who commit more serious offenses may be tried in the U.S. District Court at Phoenix, Arizona.

PARK INTERPRETIVE SERVICE

In Grand Canyon, as in the other scenic areas of the National Park System, there is a varied interpretive program that will surely help you to greater knowledge and understanding of both the natural and the human history of the Parks. The program includes exhibits at the Visitor Centers, guided walks, campfire programs, informal talks, and accurate, easy-to-read literature. Specific details on the interpretive program are found in Chapters 3, 4, and 8. Remember that Park naturalists, who are also in uniform, are the Parks' interpretive force. They are here to help you understand what you see in the Parks, and they are responsible for all interpretive services, which are free of charge. The wise visitor plans to take part in some, if not all, of the naturalist activities.

HOW TO REACH THE PARK

Grand Canyon National Park is located in the northwestern section of Arizona in Coconino County. (The Park is *not* the boundary between Utah and Arizona. All of the Grand Canyon is within the State of Arizona.) The Park can be reached by automobile, train, bus, or airplane. Bus, train, and airline schedule information is available from your local travel agent or from Fred Harvey or the Utah Parks Company (see page 169 for addresses).

By Automobile. Major highways serving the Park are U.S. 66 (Interstate 40), which is approximately 60 miles south of the South Rim, and U.S. 89, which is approximately 30 miles east of the Desert View, or eastern boundary of the Park. Automobile associations, touring services, travel bureaus, chambers of commerce, and gasoline stations can furnish road information and maps.

Access to the *South Rim* from the west is made by turning north from U.S. 66 near Williams onto Arizona Route 64 to Grand Canyon Village (59 miles). From the east, turn north off U.S. 66 at Flagstaff and take U.S. 180 to Grand Canyon Village (79 miles). Or take U.S. 89 to Cameron (51 miles). From the north, take U.S. 89 to Cameron, and then go west on Arizona Route 64 to Grand Canyon Village. Regardless of the weather, roads on and to the South Rim of the Park are kept open all year, with the possible exception of periods of only a few hours' duration.

To get to the *North Rim* by car from the South Rim, take Arizona Route 64 from Grand Canyon Village to Cameron (57 miles), thence north and west on U.S. 89 and 89A to Jacob Lake (115 miles), and then drive south on Arizona Route 67 to North Rim headquarters (45 miles)—total distance, 217 miles. (It is only 10 air-miles between these two points, or 20.6 miles via cross-canyon trail.) From U.S. 66 near Flagstaff, take U.S. 89 and 89A to Jacob Lake (164 miles). From Zion National Park, take Utah Route 15 and U.S. 89 and 89A to Jacob Lake (79 miles). From Bryce Canyon National Park, take Utah Route 12 and U.S. 89 and 89A to Jacob Lake (117 miles). The road from Jacob Lake to the North Rim is closed by snow from about mid-October to mid-May.

By Bus. Year-round bus service is available to the South Rim by Nava-Hopi Tours at Flagstaff; and Fred Harvey bus at Williams.

11

North Rim bus service is available usually from June 15 through Labor Day via Utah Parks Company bus from Lund, Utah, through Cedar City, and Zion and Bryce Canyon National Parks.

By Train. Railway service is available to the South Rim year-round by Santa Fe Railroad, although passenger trains all the way to the South Rim Village are available only during summer. (This branch is the only rail service that enters any National Park directly.) Train passengers are brought to the South Rim by bus from Williams Junction during winter, spring, and fall.

The closest rail service to North Rim is through Lund, Utah, on the Union Pacific Railroad, where bus connections are provided by Utah Parks Company during summer only.

By Airplane. The airport at Flagstaff (80 miles—Nava-Hopi Tours bus to South Rim) is serviced by daily flights of Frontier Airlines. Throughout the year, there are also daily flights of Bonanza Air Lines from Salt Lake City, Las Vegas, and Phoenix to the Grand Canyon Airport (8 miles south of Grand Canyon Village on Arizona Route 64). Fred Harvey buses meet all Bonanza flights and return. Private airplanes may also land at this airport. Rental cars are available at Flagstaff or Grand Canyon Airport.

Bonanza Airlines has flights going to Cedar City, Utah, where bus connections are provided (by special arrangement) by Utah Parks Company to the North Rim during the summer only.

The Grand Canyon Flying Service, based at Grand Canyon Airport, and the Tusayan Helicopter Flights, Inc., based nearby, will fly you from the South Rim to the North Rim and back, during the summer, for a memorable look at the Canyon or will pick you up at the North Rim. On the North Rim, they use a Forest Service landing strip just outside the Park boundary. Arrangements can be made at Grand Canyon Airport or at the transportation desks at the hotels and lodges.

ENTRANCE FEES

Grand Canyon National Park has been designated as a recreation fee area pursuant to the Land and Water Conservation Fund Act of 1965.

12

1. *Annual Recreation/Conservation Sticker*—This $7.00 permit admits the individual paying such fee and all those who accompany him in a private noncommercial automobile. This permit is good until March 31 of the year following issuance and admits the purchaser and passengers in the car to all National Parks, National Forests, and other federal areas designated as "recreation fee areas."

2. *Daily and 30-Day Permits*—Shorter-period permits are available, but exact fees vary. For information inquire at Park entrance stations. All of the above permits are authorized by the Land and Water Conservation Fund Act of 1965.

CLIMATE AND THE GRAND CANYON

The Grand Canyon may be visited any day in the year. When other mountain resorts are snowed-in, the titan of chasms is easily accessible. During the winter, snow falls in the pine forest along the rim, and the upper sections of the trails to the river are covered with a white blanket. Nevertheless, one may venture muleback down the two principal trails, confident that spring soon will begin to peek out timidly and early summer appear just around the turn. For, going down, the climate changes perceptibly every few hundred feet, so that when on the Rim a nipping frost is in the air, there are fragile desert flowers blooming along the river gulches.

South Rim. Mild temperatures, with a minimum of precipitation may be expected on the South Rim during the months of May, June, September, and October. Thundershowers are usually frequent occurrences during July and August, particularly in the afternoon. The first snow of the season may be expected in late October or early November and brief periods of inclement weather may continue through late April. However, roads on and to the South Rim of the Park are kept open all year, with the possible exception of periods of only a few hours' duration. The majority of winter days are cool and sunny.

North Rim. Roads to the North Rim are usually closed by snow from October 15, or shortly thereafter, until about mid-May. June, July, August, and September are normally pleasant, with cool nights,

Data, Precipitation and Temperature
(10-year average)

TEMPERATURES

	Jan.	Feb.	March	April	May	June	July	Aug.	Sept.	Oct.	Nov.	Dec.
SOUTH RIM												
Mean Maximum	41	45	51	61	71	81	85	81	77	66	51	45
Mean Minimum	20	22	25	32	39	47	54	53	47	38	27	21
NORTH RIM												
Mean Maximum	35	39	46	52	62	74	77	74	69	59	46	40
Mean Minimum	12	9	19	25	34	41	47	46	39	31	25	14
INNER CANYON												
Mean Maximum	56	62	70	89	89	101	106	101	96	86	59	50
Mean Minimum	36	40	46	56	60	71	79	74	70	59	41	29

MONTHLY PRECIPITATION NORMALS

	Jan.	Feb.	March	April	May	June	July	Aug.	Sept.	Oct.	Nov.	Dec.
SOUTH RIM	1.31	1.47	1.23	0.72	0.60	0.70	1.05	2.35	1.30	1.16	0.74	1.15
NORTH RIM	3.79	3.51	3.82	1.94	1.31	1.02	1.55	3.57	1.23	1.55	1.37	3.88
INNER CANYON	0.55	0.69	0.66	0.38	0.22	0.38	0.78	1.22	0.43	0.49	0.52	0.46

thundershowers being most frequent during July and August. Sudden snowstorms occurring any time after the first of October may inconvenience visitors who stay on the North Rim after that date.

As you can see from the data shown in the chart on page 14, the weather in July or August is not torrid, except at the very bottom of the giant cleft. Up on top the Rim is almost a mile and a half above sea level. Maximum shade temperature on the Rim seldom exceeds 85°, though it may be twenty degrees or so warmer far down below. Mornings, evenings, and nights are cool and dry. The difference of nearly a mile in altitude between the Colorado River and Canyon Rim is like traveling hundreds of miles north or south on the level.

Off-season visits to Grand Canyon are especially rewarding. From November to March, the Park is uncrowded, and accommodations and most sightseeing trips are readily available. The roads are open all year, and the weather is mostly sunny and pleasant. The Canyon's wintry color moods are the most spectacular, especially when sparkling snow cover the Rim's ramparts.

What to Wear. No special clothing—except suitable coats for cool evenings—is required in summer, as long as the visitor does not plan to leave the Rim. Warm clothing is necessary in winter. Good hiking boots are needed by those who plan to hike extensively along the Rim or down into the Canyon. Further information on hiking gear can be found on page 86.

Chapter 2.

The Grand Canyon Through the Ages

ROADSIDE erosion is familiar to us all. The rain falling in the plowed field forms rivulets in the furrows. The rivulets unite in a muddy torrent in the roadside gutter. With succeeding showers the gutter wears an ever-deepening channel in the soft soil. With the passing season the gutter becomes a gully. Here and there, in places, its banks undermine and fall in. Here and there the rivulets from the field wear tiny tributary gullies. Between the breaks in the banks and the tributaries, irregular masses of earth remain standing, sometimes resembling mimic cliffs, sometimes washed and worn into mimic peaks and spires.

A hundred times we have idly noted the fantastic water-carved walls and minareted slopes of these ditches. But seldom, perhaps, have we realized that the muddy roadside ditch and the world-famous Grand Canyon of Arizona are, from nature's standpoint, identical; they differ only in soil and size.

According to most geologists, the Kaibab Plateau and several other uplifted areas in northern Arizona were formed during the Laramide Revolution (the time when the present Rocky Mountains were being formed—about 60 to 28 million years ago). The ancestral Colorado River, flowing from the northeast, was deflected by the uplift and flowed in a southeasterly direction. During mid-Cenozoic time (about 12 million years ago), a rising land mass in eastern Arizona blocked the southeasterly flow of this stream which in turn created an inland lake of several hundred square miles. Deposits of this lake, found today, are known as the Bidahochi formation. Meanwhile on the west side of the Kaibab Plateau a system of small drainages was beginning to coalesce to form one main drainage which captured the waters of the ancestral Colorado River drainage system and began the erosion which created the Grand Canyon of today. The carving

16

Riders on the Kaibab Trail go through a tunnel approaching the Kaibab Suspension Bridge. This bridge is the only safe crossing of the Colorado River within the Park. Fred Harvey photo.

of the Canyon took place sometime during the period from about 10 million to about 2 million years ago.

The river has really itself cut only a narrow slot. The great width of the Grand Canyon is the result of landslides, of water from melting snows, and especially from violent summer thunderstorms draining into the canyon from the sides, and of the other usual agents of erosion such as wind, ice, and frost.

The resulting rock debris—boulders, gravel, sand, and mud—has been working its way downhill to the river. Hence the widening process has been supplying the Colorado's waters, flowing along at an average of 5 to 7 miles an hour, with cutting tools—sand for scouring, boulders for pounding. Year after year these tools have helped to deepen the gorge still further. You can get an idea of what a mighty river the Colorado is when you learn that it is the fifth longest river in the United States—nearly 2,000 miles. It has its source in North Central Colorado in Rocky Mountain National Park and it is joined by the Green in Canyonlands National Park in Utah which rises in the Wind River Mountains of Wyoming. Along its course to the Gulf of California in Mexico, the Colorado cuts nineteen major canyons, the Grand Canyon being the largest.

In the Grand Canyon the river averages about 300 feet in width but has a maximum depth of 66 feet. At the Kaibab Suspension Bridge the depth varies from 12 to 45 feet and it flows along at speeds from 2½ to 20 miles per hour. In the Park, the Colorado has no falls, but has many rapids in the Canyon. (There are about 200 main rapids in the river between Lee's Ferry and Lake Mead.) It drops a total of 1,850 feet in the Grand Canyon, averaging nine feet per mile. Over the years, the Colorado's raging brown or red torrents carry past any given point in the Canyon an average of half a million tons of mud and sand every 24 hours! In addition, its waters have probably swept a nearly equal load of boulders along the river bottom. Now, because of the closing of Glen Canyon Dam upstream from Grand Canyon, the impounded waters of Lake Powell retain much of this silt and sand. This has had a considerable clearing effect on the water as it flows through the Canyon. The Glen Canyon Dam has also had a slight cooling effect on the water, but by regulating the flow of the river, there are no longer the extreme high- and low-water levels that existed in the past. Hoover Dam, located 267 miles downstream from the mouth of Bright Angel Creek, has no effect on the Canyon since it backs up the water 115 miles at high-water mark which forms the upper end of Lake Mead some 80 miles below the western boundary of the Park.

In cutting this world-renowned chasm, which measures roughly 217 miles long (105 river miles of which are in the National Park), the Colorado River has exposed a great series of rock layers. From many points you can see fine examples of the rocks of all the known

18

eras of geological time—from the Precambrian to the present era, the Cenozoic—a span of nearly two billion years. Few places in the world permit such a complete geologic story.

GRAND CANYON'S GEOLOGIC STORY

Geological Record in the Canyon goes back to when the earth was still molten, but cooling to form its sturdy crust of granite and gneiss. This first era leaves no evidence of any primordial life for over a billion years, not even a single fossil. But gradually the earth cooled, atmosphere formed, and water vapor condensed into rain.

During this first era of time, too, there existed in this region a mighty mountain range. During succeeding ages, this mountain range wore away by erosion to an almost completely level plain. Then the region slipped beneath an ancient sea. Sediment formed in the sea, became hardened and formed a layer of limestone. Then the land rose out of the sea, to a point comparatively low above sea level. Another layer of rock was built upon the top of the limestone by ancient rivers, which carried mud along as the mighty Colorado—which cut the Grand Canyon—does today.

Mighty stresses and strains then caused the earth's crust to break into gigantic rock blocks, which, tilted by the stupendous hand of Nature, became a range of mountains, thousands of feet high. Ages passed and the mountains wore down to an almost completely level plain once more, leaving the rock formations exposed, like great islands. Then the region was submerged. The sand deposited in the sea formed a layer of what is known as Tapeats sandstone. That was the beginning of the Paleozoic times, the era of ancient life.

Upon the Tapeats sandstone, in later time, many rock layers were deposited in seas or on land until the end of the great Paleozoic geological era, some 230 million years ago. Today, we can identify in the upper walls thick layers of limestone derived from deposits in prehistoric seas, shales derived from muds, and sandstones derived from sands. In these rock layers are remnants of prehistoric life. First, primitive plantlife in the sea; then, as we examine younger and hence higher layers in the Grand Canyon walls, we see primitive fossil seashells and crablike trilobites. Later and higher, traces of more advanced forms successively appear: armored fish, which were among

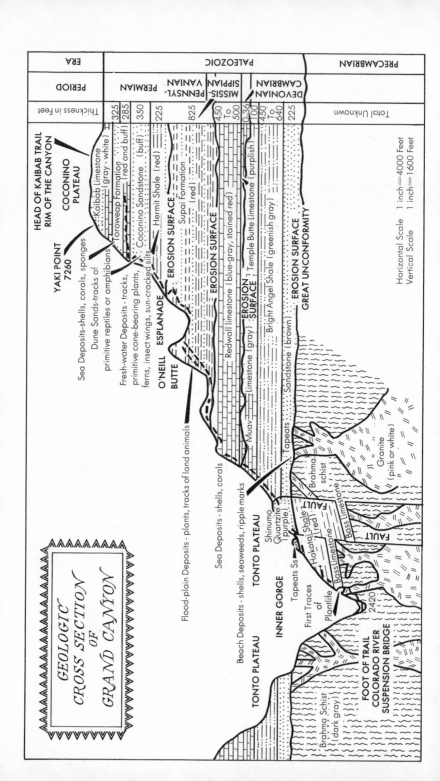

GEOLOGIC
CROSS SECTION
OF
GRAND CANYON

Horizontal Scale 1 inch = 4000 Feet
Vertical Scale 1 inch = 1600 Feet

ERA	PERIOD	Thickness in Feet		
PALEOZOIC	PERMIAN	325	Kaibab Limestone (gray - white)	HEAD OF KAIBAB TRAIL RIM OF THE CANYON — COCONINO PLATEAU
		285	Toroweap Formation (red and buff)	YAKI POINT 7260
		350	Coconino Sandstone (buff)	Sea Deposits-shells, corals, sponges
		225	Hermit Shale (red)	Dune Sands-tracks of primitive reptiles or amphibians
	PENNSYL- VANIAN	825	Supai Formation (red)	Fresh-water Deposits - tracks, primitive cone-bearing plants, ferns, insect wings, sun-cracked silts
	MISSIS- SIPPIAN	450 To 500	Redwall limestone (blue-gray, stained red)	EROSION SURFACE — O'NEILL ESPLANADE
	DEVONIAN	0-30	Limestone (gray)	EROSION SURFACE — EROSION SURFACE — BUTTE
	CAMBRIAN	100	Temple Butte Limestone (purplish)	Flood-plain Deposits - plants, tracks of land animals
		450 To 640	Muav Limestone (gray)	
			Bright Angel Shale (greenish gray)	Sea Deposits - shells, corals
		225	Tapeats Sandstone (brown)	EROSION SURFACE
PRECAMBRIAN	DEVONIAN	Total Unknown		GREAT UNCONFORMITY

Granite (pink or white)

Brahma schist

Shinumo Quartzite (purple)

Hakatai Shale (red)

Bass Limestone

FAULT

TONTO PLATEAU

INNER GORGE

TONTO PLATEAU

First Traces of Plantlife

Tapeats Ss

Beach Deposits - shells, seaweeds, ripple marks

Sea Deposits - shells, corals

Brahma Schist (dark gray)

FOOT OF TRAIL
COLORADO RIVER
SUSPENSION BRIDGE
2420

FAULT

the first creatures with backbones; and next the early kinds of land life—fine fossil ferns, and remains of salamanderlike and lizardlike reptiles. This was the Upper Permian Period, or the "Age of Amphibians."

What about the two following eras? The Mesozoic, era of medieval life, a hundred and forty million years long, the "Age of Reptiles"— of the great land monsters, the dinosaurs, and the flying reptiles. The Cenozoic, era of modern life, the age of man, of modern animals and plants. Vermilion Cliffs to the north, Cedar Mountain, east of Desert View, and Red Butte, south of the Canyon, are Mesozoic remnants. The Pine Mountains, 85 miles west, and the San Francisco Peaks, near Flagstaff, represent the Cenozoic. All the rest has been swept away by the Colorado and its tributaries as they cut the Grand Canyon. They were, in fact, the river's tools—every grain of sand, every frost-shattered boulder, every mountain peak. Even as the Canyon carving went on, volcanic activity near Toroweap Point in the Grand Canyon National Monument caused lava to flow into the Canyon, forming what is known today as Lava Falls.

This, then, is the story of Grand Canyon—the geological record of an earth *at least* two billion years old, nearly three-quarters of which had transpired before the first record of life, and all but one million years before man came into existence.

GRAND CANYON'S ROCK FORMATIONS

Standing on either Rim, one can easily read the fascinating chronicle of antiquity from the walls of the Canyon and the sides of its buttes and temples. Actually the different rock strata, or beds, encountered by the Colorado River as it cut downward are controlling factors in the development of the Grand Canyon. The younger beds were worn away first and gradually older and older beds were exposed underneath. A detailed knowledge of the sequence of formation is not required for understanding Grand Canyon scenery. It is sufficient to know that basically there are three great series that have been designated by terms descriptive of their position in the Canyon. The upper and younger strata lie nearly horizontal forming the walls of the Outer Canyon and are referred to as "the Horizontal Series." Beneath the Horizontal Series in numerous places are tilted blocks of strata or rock formations that are referred to as "the Wedge

Series." Underneath the formation of the Horizontal and Wedge Series is the basement of old schists and granites that may be termed "the Vertical Series." This series of old rock forms the walls of the Inner Gorge.

THE OUTER CANYON

At the top of the Outer Canyon is the great forest-covered plateau, which at the edge of the Canyon terminates in cliffs of grayish-white, slabby limestone. This has been named Kaibab limestone from the great plateau which it constitutes on the north side of the Canyon; it also constitutes the Coconino Plateau of the South Rim. This limestone formation averages about 325 feet thick and, while nearly uniform in character from top to bottom, contains harder and softer beds and many layers of flint. It also contains remains of an ancient seal life—shells, corals, and sponges. Teeth of sharks have also been found. When these animals lived here about 200 million years ago—a great body of salt water extended at least several hundred miles in every direction. It is believed to have been an extension of the ocean to the west. The presence of corals and sharks' teeth suggests that this was a warm sea.

Next below the Kaibab limestone is the Toroweap formation which embraces red and buff sandstones at top and bottom with intermediate gray limestones. It was deposited under marine conditions and reaches a thickness of up to 300 feet in the Canyon.

Under this is a stratum of Coconino sandstone which is a massive, white to buff, crossbedded sandstone to about 400 feet in depth in some places. These inclined surfaces, readily seen in cliff faces, apparently represent the lee sides of sand dunes. The Coconino sandstone is considered to have been derived principally from sand piled up by the action of wind in an extensive area bordering the sea. Trails of quadrupedal animals, small primitive reptiles, or amphibians have been found on crossbed surfaces. The name of this formation comes from the Coconino Plateau to the south, whose rim is more than a thousand feet lower than that of the Kaibab.

Next below the Coconino sandstone is the red shale of the Hermit Formation which ranges from 100 to 300 feet in thickness. It is an accumulation of mud and fine sandy material deposited ages ago by streams flowing into this region from the northeast. Here and there

22

are evidences of former pools and arroyos with wavy ripple marks on their borders and a thin film of shiny slime covering the surface. Trails of worms, footprints of small salamanderlike animals, and impressions of ferns are found delicately preserved in this slime. Raindrop impressions, molds of salt crystals, and numerous sun cracks also add to the picture of this ancient period.

The Supai formation, which is about 800 feet thick in the Grand Canyon, is composed of alternating layers of hard sandstone and soft shale (hardened mud). The red materials are believed to have been brought into this region by ancient rivers from former granitic highlands far to the northeast and to have been deposited on a great flood plain. The climate in this region was at that time probably rather arid; the vegetation consisted principally of ferns and related plants, and the animals included a group of large but primitive four-footed creatures. Some of the tracks of the animals may be seen in the sandstone a little farther down the trail. These red and red-brown rocks constitute a large part of many fine promontories and ridges projecting far out into the Canyon. Such features as O'Neill Butte, Rama Shrine, Geikie Peak, Isis Temple, Lyell Butte, Tower of Set, Newton Butte, Apollo Temple, Sagittarius Ridge, Venus Temple, Tower of Ra, Dana Butte, Horus Temple, and Krishna Shrine, consist of the Supai formation. It also constitutes the great red steps of the middle slopes of the gigantic ridges Vishnu Temple, Shiva Temple, Zoroaster Temple, Wotan's Throne, Osiris Temple, Brahma Temple, and other prominent features. Incidentally, François E. Matthes, who was in charge of making the United States Geological Survey topographic map of the Grand Canyon in 1902-03, is responsible for naming of many of the promontories and ridges after mythological deities, Oriental religious orders as well as for those named for southwestern Indian tribes. The derivation of many of the Grand Canyon's place names are given on pages 186-192.

Almost everywhere below these red beds is a great wall due to the Redwall limestone, a massive body of hard compact limestone up to 500 feet thick. It is a pale blue-gray when fresh or broken, but most of the cliffs are stained red (iron oxides) by wash from the overlying red beds. This stain gives the surface of the rock a very misleading reddish appearance from which the name Redwall originated. The great cliff of this limestone is a very conspicuous feature throughout the Canyon and always appears in regular order in the

23

succession of formations. It also constitutes many long flat-topped spurs and buttresses extending out from the Supai-capped promontories, and outlying masses of the Redwall limestone isolated by erosion. The formation can be seen in Newberry Butte, Solomon Temple, Cheops Temple, Sheba Temple, and many other flat-topped buttes and mesas. The top of the limestone ledge is marked by a narrow bench at the foot of the Supai slope, and in many places the cliff shows deep alcoves or recesses with overhanging roof. Redwall limestone, itself, was formed beneath a sea which extended over this region from far to the north. In it are fossils representing many types of ocean life, such as sea shells, corals, and sections of sea lilies. Parts of it are composed almost entirely of the limy skeletons of such animals. The purity of the limestone indicates that it was formed in clear, quiet water, probably at the bottom of a relatively deep sea.

Below the Redwall limestone lies the Temple Butte limestone. These small patches of lavender rock—0 to 36 feet in thickness—represent the age when fishes were the highest type of life known on earth. During that period, called the Devonian Period, sand and lime deposits were formed over this area by fresh waters, filling in many stream channels which had been cut in what was then the surface rock. Today, numerous isolated patches of this material can be found in the walls of Grand Canyon, and in these have been discovered the remains of strange types of primitive fish that lived in the waters of that ancient period.

The Muav formation consists largely of gray limestones and varies in thickness from 50 feet at the east to 400 feet at the west end of the Canyon. This limestone originated beneath the sea. The sandstone and shale, which can be seen immediately below as the wide benchlike platform, represent the same general period, but they were formed on a beach and in shallow water, respectively. Obviously, therefore, this region was gradually sinking at that time, so that the sea became deeper as the lime of the Muav limestone was deposited. In this limestone have been found the shells of numerous types of primitive sea animals.

The Bright Angel formation is a greenish-gray shale that ranges

---

Looking north from the Canyon Rim from point a few hundred yards east of Hopi Point up Bright Angel Creek to North Rim. National Park Service photo.

from 200 to 650 feet in thickness. It was once mud on the bottom of a shallow sea and in it have been found some of the oldest known types of animal life. Small sea shells, the skeletons of primitive crablike animals, and the borings of worms are preserved in great numbers in some parts of this formation. The remains of many of these animals occur in rocks of similar age far to the north, indicating that a great inland sea covered this entire area during that ancient period, some 430 to 500 million years ago.

The shelf, or platform, eroded in the Bright Angel shale is known as the Tonto Plateau. It is one of the characteristic topographic features of the lower part of the Outer Canyon. An old Indian trail follows it for many miles on the south side of the river. Although the trail is not used much by man, it is in many places maintained as a recognizable way of passage by wild burros. Below the Bright Angel shale is the Tapeats sandstone, lowest and oldest formation of the Horizontal Series and the Paleozoic Era. It forms a precipitous cliff at the outer boundary of the Inner Gorge and the lower boundary of the Outer Canyon. It is rather dark brown in color and averages about 200 feet in thickness in the Grand Canyon.

The stepped topography of the Outer Grand Canyon, as previously stated, is due to the fortuitous alternation of rock formation having widely different resistance to erosion. Also, by chance, there is an alternation of light-colored formations and dark-colored formations, with intermediate red formations. The colors, which are caused chiefly by the oxides of various minerals are generally subdued, yet they have extensive distribution in horizontal pattern. They interest the eye whether seen in the contrast of bright sunlight and deep shadow of midday or in the soft, diffused light of sunrise and sunset. The various formations or stratas are not at the same height everywhere, due to fractures, or "faults," in the formations, along which the rocks on one side are much lower than on the other.

As the land rose and the rock strata fractured and faulted under the stress and strain, side canyons to the main gorge were also formed. Bright Angel Canyon, for instance, was caused by a large fault that occurred in northeast to southwest direction and the displacement along the fault in this area ranges from 150 to 180 feet. Water draining from the North Rim easily eroded the fractured rock along the fault to form the Canyon and since the land slopes away from the South Rim carrying the water away from the Grand Canyon, that end of the fault eroded much less rapidly. This process has happened many times and in many places within the Grand Canyon and has determined the location of most of the side canyons, and contributed to the isolation of temples, buttes, and other picturesque forms.

Faulting is a major factor in the Wedge Series, too. As the uplifting of the land continued, the Colorado River deepened its channel, and the Outer Grand Canyon expanded in size. At last the river cut through the Horizontal Series in places and impinged on high mounts formed by tilted members of the Wedge Series. These wedges—of strata downdropped on faults—occur at various places in the Grand Canyon. They are next to the oldest group of rocks and are much older than the Horizontal Series above.

The largest area of the Wedge Series lies adjacent to the big bend of the Colorado River at the east end of the Park. It may be seen to the north of Desert View. Here the beds are relatively soft and uniformly bedded sandstone and shale. In the broad Lava Creek and Nankoweap Creek basins smoothly rounded slopes are eroded on the Chuar Series. Its cream to buff color produces a light expanse. The underlying Dox formation is generally a brick red. Above it is a thick series of black lava flows that form an imposing cliff.

Beneath the Dox is a massive hardened sandstone, the Shinumo quartzite, which stands in sheer cliffs of purple rock. The quartzite strongly resists erosion and often forms hills on the ancient land surface cut after faulting of the Wedge Series. Beneath the Shinumo is the Hakatai shale, a thin-bedded, bench-forming sequence of the most vividly colored strata in the Canyon. Some of the beds are bright vermilion, while others are deep red. Beneath them is the cliff-forming Bass limestone which weathers to a dark chocolate brown. These ledges of limestone with wavy markings on the surface were formed hundreds of millions of years ago by the action of primitive calcium-secreting algae. Such plants are abundantly represented today and in many areas are causing lime to be deposited in the form of stony structures known as reefs, which are similar in most respects to the ones seen today as ledges in the walls of Grand Canyon. These fossils are considered to be some of the oldest definite traces of life known.

As described on page 89, the Kaibab trail descends from the Tonto platform to the Inner Gorge at the suspension bridge on downdropped blocks of the Wedge Series. A large area may be seen above the Inner Gorge west of Bright Angel Canyon. Other wedges occur in Bright Angel and Phantom Canyons and in the Ottoman and Hindu amphitheaters. Except north from Lipan Point to Desert View, the Wedge Series is not very conspicuous or important as a landscape element. It provides only a local variation in the structural and color patterns.

THE INNER GORGE

The Colorado River, cutting through the Vertical Series and isolated blocks of the Wedge Series, began to erode the narrow canyon known as the Inner Gorge (or Granite Gorge). It has precipitous walls and just a few miles above the mouth of Bright Angel Creek is about 1500 feet deep although only 1700 feet wide. (The Inner Gorge is higher than the Empire State Building.) It extends for miles through the central part of the Park with a depth of 1000 feet below the Tonto platform near the base of the Horizontal Series.

As the name implies, the Vertical Series consists of rock layers standing on end. They are mostly ancient sediments and lavas which were so changed by heat and pressure when buried deep that the original features were almost obliterated. They have been invaded by molten granite and have soaked up granitic emanations until it is sometimes difficult to tell whether original rock or granite is present in greater quantity. The metamorphosed ancient sediments (Vishnu and Brahma schist) weather to dark gray, brownish-black, and black. These dark rocks were long ago upturned and badly shattered. They are the roots of mountains, the upper parts of which were worn away. The great alternations of texture and mineralogical composition could have developed only under conditions of pressure and heat requiring an overlying mantle of rock many thousands of feet in thickness. The great covering mass was present as an elevated region that since has been washed away. The folding into mountains and their subsequent removal represent the story of the first era of geologic history in this region.

The nearly vertical, light-colored or pink bands seen in the dark rocks of the Inner Gorge are granites—formed in cracks or fissures. Close examination of the granite shows that it differs in texture from volcanic rocks in that it is composed of large crystals of various minerals such as can be formed only by slow cooling far beneath the earth's surface. Volcanic lavas which flow out on the surface cool so rapidly that no large crystals are formed. The presence of these

28

granites in the Inner Gorge of Grand Canyon is evidence that great masses of rock, now worn away, once covered this region. The granite, geologists say, is about one billion three hundred and fifty million years old.

The various rocks of the Vertical Series are all very hard and all are resistant to erosion. From the standpoint of cutting and abrasion they are essentially homogeneous. So the walls of the Inner Gorge are uniformly steep and precipitous, not stepped like those of the Outer Canyon. Except where tributary streams have deposited great boulder deltas, there are few places where a person can walk or even stand along the river. Actually, the Inner Gorge is a dark and somber place. Except at midday, the shadows are long and continuous. In the vicinity of the rock deltas, great rapids make a constant roar that reverberates through adjacent parts of the Canyon.

GEOLOGY OF GRAND CANYON NATIONAL MONUMENT

The geological history and origin of the Monument is similar to that of Grand Canyon National Park, but adds to it a more recent chapter of volcanic activity. After the principal topographic features of the area had been developed and the side canyons cut to almost their present depth, volcanic activity began. Great quantities of intensely hot molten lava poured forth from the sixty or more volcanic craters of the region, down the slopes, thereby changing the original topography and building a mountain range—the Pine Mountains—approximately 30 miles long. Of prime importance to students of geology is this volcanic activity on the Monument. There is evidence that at one time the outpouring of molten lava flowed down the north wall of Grand Canyon and dammed the old Toroweap Canyon and the Colorado River in the Grand Canyon.

Remnants of this dam and lava slides may be seen on the Grand Canyon walls below the volcanic cone of Vulcan's Throne. This lava, and that from other unnamed volcanic cones to the west pouring into the Inner Gorge of Grand Canyon, choked the Colorado River channel and formed a dam, behind which a lake was formed. The large amount of water flowing down the Colorado River, carrying tremendous quantities of sand, silt, and gravel, began the process of cutting down through this lava dam. The remains of the lava dam

29

may be seen today on both sides of the river in the Inner Gorge. So remarkable was this feature that Major Powell made note of it about a hundred years ago, and other early geologists who came later also mention it.

In the case of Toroweap Valley, conditions differed. The amount of water coming down through the prehistoric Toroweap Canyon had never been large and it was totally inadequate to cut through the lava dam at its mouth. On the other hand, the waste material from the bordering cliffs and the material carried down by flood waters at the upper end have been slowly but steadily filling up the old canyon, until today we recognize it as Toroweap Valley. The thickness of this fill, in all probability, averages several hundred feet throughout the greater part of the valley. At its mouth, this fill may be as much as 2,000 feet thick.

It has been a little over four hundred years since white men first saw the Grand Canyon. This is not a significant period when contrasted with geological time which reckons years by the hundreds of millions. Hence to present-day man, change in the physiography of the Grand Canyon is negligible or nonexistent. The canyon undoubtedly looked very much as it does today when Columbus sailed from Spain, when Rome was founded, when Troy fell, when Hammurabi wrote the laws of Babylon. And it will still be substantially the same two thousand years in the future. Man need not be concerned.

Chapter 3.

Exploring the Rims of the Canyon

To fully appreciate the Grand Canyon, everyone should visit both the North and South Rims. Actually, Grand Canyon has often been called the "two-in-one National Park," because the variance in seasons and natural endowments is so greatly different between the two Rims. Even the range of problems presented by them makes the Grand Canyon a fascinating place for the people that live and work there.

GETTING TO KNOW THE SOUTH RIM

The South Rim of Grand Canyon is on a flat, pine-forested plateau. Averaging 6,000 to 7,000 feet above sea level, it looks across to the higher North Rim, which geologically is part of the same plateau. Relatively mild winters and greater accessibility make the South Rim the more visited side.

SOUTH RIM ROADS

There are two major drives along the South Rim. One leads eastward toward the Painted Desert, and it reveals magnificent views from Yavapai, Yaki, Grandview, Moran, and Lipan Points. The gamut of changes in canyon architecture is climaxed at Desert View with a last long sight of the Colorado River. The road to the west takes you past Grand Canyon Village and the hotels. As you continue along, glimpses are caught of the river's erratic course, twisting at the feet of rainbow-colored ramparts, from such spots as Maricopa, Hopi, Mohave and Pima Points, and Hermit's Rest. *Maximum* speed on Park roads is 45 m.p.h., except where posted. Drive carefully.

The East Rim Drive. The starting point of your journey toward the east may be the Park Headquarters and Visitor Center. Housed here are fascinating exhibits that tell the story of the Canyon in dioramas, photographs, and exhibits. Its four sections—geology, animal life, Indians, and discovery—describe in simple and enjoyable fashion how the Canyon came to be, what forms of life have inhabited it, and how it has been explored. And if you still have questions after you have seen all there is to see, a Park Naturalist will be glad to answer them for you.

After leaving the Visitor Center, heading toward Desert View, the first point of interest you reach is Yavapai Point (elevation 7,073 feet). From it you can see down the Grand Canyon to the west as far as Powell Plateau and to the east as far as Comanche Point. From Yavapai (named for the Yavapai Indians of Arizona) two glimpses of the River are seen—neither of them extended nor inspiring. Pipe Creek is in the lateral canyon at the right, while to the left you see the Redwall under the Battleship with its huge amphitheaters.

To the east from Yavapai is Yaki Point 1½ miles away, presenting the full succession of geological strata down to the granite. Toward its base are bold cliffs of Redwall limestone, rising to a long promontory of red beds of the Supai formation which culminates in a peak known as O'Neill Butte. Beyond O'Neill Butte can be seen Newton Butte with its flat top of red sandstone of the Supai formation and Lyell Butte, another Supai outlier, can be seen a little farther down the Canyon. Newton Butte lies below Shoshone Point, another promontory on the Coconino Plateau, and is separated from O'Neill Butte by Cremation Creek Canyon. The great summit wall in the distance to the east is at the western edge of the Painted Desert through which the Little Colorado River has cut its canyon.

Looking north across the Grand Canyon, probably the most conspicuous feature is Buddha Temple, capped by the hard basal bed of the Kaibab limestone. Manu Temple, behind it to the right, and Isis Temple, in front of it to the left, have lost this resistant layer and the Coconino sandstone is rounding away as a result of rain and other erosive agents. Zoroaster, Brahma, and Deva Temples, the great structures that flank Bright Angel Creek on the east, still re-

The view of the Canyon from Yavapai Point. Fred Harvey photo.

tain a capping of this resistant limestone. In Cheops Pyramid the Coconino and Supai beds also have been removed and this tabular mass of the Redwall limestone has been separated from the main ledges of the formation by erosion.

Looking northeast there is a myriad of gigantic sculptured masses. Wotan's Throne dominates. It is the central feature of a great ridge extending south from Walhalla Plateau at Cape Royal, with an intricate series of branching ridges exhibiting a marvelous assemblage of notable forms.

One of the major points of interest at Yavapai Point is the Museum. Here much of the Canyon story and the history of the earth's existence is bared to you. Its tale, told by a Park Naturalist and illustrated with a huge topographical map, exhibits, and a battery of binoculars, will convey within an hour a deeper understanding of the miracle of the ages that produced the chasm. For instance, the binoculars in fixed position are directed at certain spots in the Canyon. A card below each set describes what you see. From this spot, if you have your own binoculars, you may get a close-up of Phantom Ranch, the suspension bridge across the Colorado, and the North Rim, a dozen miles away. Here you may trace the Kaibab Trail from Yaki Point to the plateau, and pick up the Bright Angel Trail below.

At Mather Point a short distance farther east, there is a plaque honoring Stephen T. Mather (1867-1930), and first Director (1916-1929) of the National Park Service.

After passing the junction of U.S. 180 and Arizona Route 64, you will have many opportunities to see the Canyon from various viewpoints. The first one you reach is Yaki Point (elevation 7,286 feet). This point (the original name, O'Neill, survives only in the butte that runs off from the point) presents substantially the same vistas up and down the Canyon, the same buttes and promontories across the River, as Yavapai. You are only 1½ miles farther east in a direct line. But, at Yaki Point you get a closer view of such Canyon features as the high Walhalla Plateau, the vast Wotan's Throne, the enormous depression of the Ottoman Amphitheater, and can see in clearer outlines Comanche Point and the Painted Desert. Almost directly across the River is Zoroaster Temple. And beneath it, as well

---

Visitors viewing the Canyon from Mather Point. This point is near where the South Entrance Road first meets the South Rim. National Park Service photo.

as on both sides of the River, it is possible to note the Tonto Plateau. The Kaibab Trail—the main Rim-to-Rim route—has its South Rim start from Yaki Point.

In Cremation Canyon, below Yaki Point, the cliffs on the west side are seen to be considerably higher than those of the east wall. Careful examination shows that the horizontal layers forming its walls are not continuous at this point and that this tributary canyon follows a line of breaking. The line along which this movement has taken place is known as the Cremation Fault. (A fault occurs when the earth's crust has broken and slipped.) Actual measurement shows a vertical slip or dislocation of 230 feet for a distance of over a mile to the northwest. This is one of many breaks or faults that, like the Bright Angel Fault (see page 26), have determined the straight courses of side canyons in the Grand Canyon.

Deep in the Canyon across from Yaki Point one may observe an ancient hill of hard black rocks buried in a series of sandy brown layers. These are among the oldest rock on the North American continent.

Continuing the journey eastward, Grandview Point (elevation 7,496 feet) is the next major stop. This location, at one time, was a lively settlement when copper was king in the Canyon and relays of burros were bringing the ore up to the Rim. Later, a three-story log hotel was built here in 1892 to accommodate tourists who came in horsedrawn stages from Flagstaff. While Grandview is no longer a copper camp or even a visitors' accommodation center, it has lost nothing of its picturesqueness by the passing of time and it is one of the most heavily visited points on the South Rim.

Looking around the horizon from Gandview Point, you once again find yourself in the center of a great stone circle. It is only the pine forest at your back that seems to break up this ring. Across the River from you have the appearance of piling up with great enormity. Just over the ridge beneath the Point is a square butte with two Coconino outcrops upon its summit that has the pseudo-poetic name of Angels Gate. Farther around to the east is the lofty Vishnu Temple capped with a Kaibab fragment which is higher than the spot you are standing. Between these two Canyon features is Wotan's Throne, 200 feet higher than Grandview Point, and the

View through trees down the South Kaibab Trail below Yaki Point. National Park Service photo.

junipers and pinyons growing on its flat top are the same species that flourish here along the South Rim. A little farther to the east, on the North Rim, you can see what appears to be the end of the Walhalla Plateau in what is called Cape Final. This is, of course, merely a promontory on the north wall thrown into sky relief by your position on Grandview. Under it, but apparently to the east of it, is a lantern-topped butte known as Jupiter Temple. Still farther to the east you can observe the Palisades of the Desert, and beyond these the long stretches of the Painted Desert.

Continuing around the horizon to the east you will note Comanche Point, on your side of the River; and then the Watchtower at Desert View, followed by Lipan, Pinal, Papago, Zuni, and Moran Points. This brings you back almost to Coronado Butte, the Three Castles, and the Sinking Ship. The latter is a small butte just east of Grandview, in which the rock layers or strata are tilted at a steep angle. Careful examination shows that these rocks are in horizontal position where they continue west under Grandview; and that in the opposite direction, or eastward from this point, they also become horizontal but are lying at much lower level. This is an interesting illustration of the bending movement in the earth's crust after these rocks were formed.

The vista to the west from Grandview is not as open due to Shoshone Point and several high ridges that lie in your line of sight. But this does not interfere with the view of the great buttes lying on either side of Bright Angel Canyon, nor the far view across the Hindu Amphitheater to Point Sublime. To the northwest, for instance, across Ottoman Amphitheater and Clear Creek Canyon are the superb series of eminences known as Zoroaster, Brahma, and Deva Temples. They are pinnacles on the ridge which extends south from Obi Point, the southwestern termination of Walhalla Plateau and beyond which flows Bright Angel Creek. These three temples are capped by outliers of Kaibab limestone, there being nearly 400 feet of this rock on Brahma Temple. Lower down and seeming very nearby in comparison, are Newberry Butte, Sheba Temple, and Solomon Temple, flat-topped mesas consisting of outliers of the Redwall limestone.

Leaving Grandview Point, you pass through tall pine trees for two miles, then descend a 600-foot hill. Ahead and to the right you

Looking northeast across the Canyon from Grandview Point. Fred Harvey photo.

38

can see the Rim of Coconino Basin—a sharp ridge extending some 15 miles. You will also pass the "Duck-on-the-Rock," an interesting rock formation. A short stop here or at Moran Point (elevation 7,157 feet) may prove to be most interesting. (The latter point was named for Thomas Moran, an artist who first visited the North Rim in 1873 with Major Powell.) Forming the bed of the Colorado River and the wide slopes on either side below Moran Point is a series of formations which lie in a tilted position. The present steep slope of these strata is the result of great movement in the earth's surface which took place before the many overlying layers of rocks were formed. Evidence of this movement is given by contrast with the horizontal layers above, which have been lifted without bending.

On the way to Desert View, you will want to make an enjoyable stop at the Tusayan Museum, four miles past Moran Point. Here exhibits deal with the development of early man, and also with the stages of human history represented by house types and pottery in the American Southwest. Other exhibits are various types of pueblo artifacts and ornaments, including materials found in the Grand Canyon and along its rims. Finally, the museum serves as a key to the partially excavated Tusayan ruin nearby. It is advisable to examine the exhibits in the order indicated, since they provide a chronological story of human history and development. The Park Naturalist in charge is glad to assist in the explanation of features in the museum and also in the ruins outside.

The nearby Tusayan Ruin, typical of many pueblo sites in the Grand Canyon region, was partially excavated in 1930. It represents a type of communal dwelling of two stories, built by Pueblo people about 1200 A.D. The ground plan forms three sides of a square with a plaza in the center. It contains four living rooms, two kivas or ceremonial chambers, and numerous storage rooms. The west side has purposely been left unexcavated in order that visitors may observe how the dwelling appeared when discovered. Numerous artifacts of various types have been found in the rooms of this ancient ruin, and they may now be seen in the Museum.

Driving eastward, your next major viewpoint is Lipan Point—the widest spot in the Canyon. Here the Colorado River forms a winding, lazy S, though when you are down close to it the water is

Duck-on-Rock as seen from a viewpoint along the East Rim Drive. Fred Harvey photo.

found to be anything but lazy. Actually, the river can be followed by eye far up to the east, disappearing for a moment behind a high ridge with a crumbling cap of sandstone for its apex, and then reappearing. Thus a rather long stretch of water is visible. To the northeast a deep gash can be detected cutting sharply across the Painted Desert. This is the canyon of the Little Colorado River which joins the main stream just beyond Cape Solitude, ten miles north of Lipan Point. At this point the Colorado River is flowing through Marble Gorge, a very steep-walled Canyon, which opens into the broader valley a few miles below the mouth of the Little Colorado. The eastern wall of this canyon, in which Comanche Point is the high spot, is, of course, the Palisades of the Desert.

It is just above the Palisades that the Colorado River leaves Marble Gorge and enters the Grand. This is really where the Grand Canyon begins. Reaching out beyond the Palisades for about 100 miles is the Painted Desert. Standing out from it the cliffs of the Little Colorado show at first, and beyond them appear the Echo Cliffs, the Mormon Ridge, Vermilion Cliffs, and Navajo Mountain. The latter is that round, blue dome which is located in Utah's Rainbow Natural Bridge country. Far to the east, almost completely blotted out by a purplish haze, you can note the outline of distant mountains.

For a quick change of scene turn for a moment and look to the west, toward Grand Canyon Village. You will observe that the horizon line will lead you around to south in a great half-circle. Here, you will note a large sunken basin in the Coconino Plateau, owing doubtless to the dip of the strata, which trend down and off toward the southeastern portion of the Painted Desert. Appearing directly over this sunken basin on the south you will see a long platform that evidently was once the normal level of the plateau. Above and beyond it appear the volcanic peaks of the San Francisco Mountains. Actually, at Lipan Point, you can look almost a mile *down* into the earth; then turn to the south and look a mile *up* to the San Francisco Peaks, or the "Home of the Gods," which is the name the Indians used because the mountains have their heads in the clouds much of the time.

The Watchtower at Desert View commands one of the most magnificent of Grand Canyon views as well as a sweeping panorama of Kaibab National Forest, the Painted Desert, and the Navajo Indian country. Fred Harvey photo.

43

Desert View (originally called Navajo Point) is two miles from Lipan Point and vistas visible from it have more variety than those from any other viewpoint along the Rim. The chief view is from the point and extends for many miles in almost every direction. While the elevation (7,488 feet) is about the same as Grandview, the Canyon here is much more open. The Inner Gorge walls are partly broken down on the south side and the slopes leading up and out are less abrupt. Across the Colorado River you will notice that the dip of the strata is from west to east, that these layers seem to be sinking and disappearing under the Palisades. This is, no doubt, responsible for the flatter effect.

Dark cliffs bordering the Colorado River below Desert View are composed of lavas that flowed out on the surface of this region long before the cutting of Grand Canyon began. Though essentially of the same composition as the much more recent volcanic rocks found on the plateau surface to the south, these lavas were formed in the second of the great divisions of time (Algonkian—Upper Precambrian —Era) represented by the rocks of this region. The muds and sands on which the molten material was poured probably formed an ancient shore line. No definite traces of animal life and only very primitive forms of plants have as yet been found in the rocks of that age. It is significant that, even in this remote period, the great processes of nature, including volcanic activity, were much the same as today.

The red shales and sandstones of Supai formation have great prominence in this portion of the canyon, especially in the ridges that bear the varied groups of "temples," "shrines" and "castles," as for example, the splendid ridges culminating in Vishnu Temple, Jupiter Temple, Siegfried Pyre, Gunther Castle, and that which bears Cardenas and Escalante Buttes at the observer's feet. The great pagoda-like mass of Vishnu Temple, to the west, and the majestic square-topped Siegfried Pyre, far to the north-northwest, bear caps of Coconino sandstone and small remnants of the lower part of the Kaibab limestone.

On Jupiter Temple, however, to the northwest, and Escalante Butte, only a thin mass of Coconino sandstone remains. In the upper wall of the canyon the persistent cliff of the Coconino sandstone is

---

A close-up of the beautiful memorial to Major John Wesley Powell and his men at Powell Point. Santa Fe Railway photo.

everywhere conspicuous, capped by the thick sheet of Kaibab limestone constituting the general plateau. Some notable projecting points of the Walhalla Plateau (which is merely a south-easterly extension of the Kaibab Plateau) are Cape Final and Cape Royal, northwest of Desert View. Wotan's Throne, still farther west, is an outlying portion of this northern plateau.

To the east of Desert View Point is a small flat-topped mesa, known as Cedar Mountain. This mesa is of especial interest in geological history, since the red sandstones and pebble rocks of which it is formed represent a remnant of widespread layers that once covered this entire region. Other remnants of these formations are found near Zion Canyon to the north, in the Painted Desert farther east, and on the plateau to the south. The rocks of Cedar Mountain contain petrified wood and other fossils similar to those from the Petrified Forest National Park.

Desert View Point received its recent name from the wonderful view of *El Desierto Pintado*—the Painted Desert. Actually, the Painted Desert is a splendid picture of color, and also the record of an interesting chapter in earth history. The rocks of the Painted Desert were formed during the age of dinosaurs. They are accumulations of pebbles, sand, mud, and lime. Logs of petrified wood, tracks of dinosaurs, and beautifully preserved fishes have been found in them. The fossil remains give some conception of the kinds of life and the climate in existence when these ancient rocks were being formed, a contrast with the life and climate of the present. The rocks of the Painted Desert lie on the surface of the youngest formations represented in Grand Canyon and belong to later geological ages.

While at Desert View you will want to visit the Watchtower. This structure, built by the Santa Fe Railway in 1932, is not an exact copy, but largely duplicates the style of early Indian towers. (While the modern one was built of native stone, steel, and concrete, the logs forming the kiva's ceiling were salvaged from the old Grandview Hotel—the first hotel ever built at the Grand Canyon.) The Watchtower (admission charge to the tower itself) contains reproductions of Indian decorations, sand paintings, and a kiva. The latter is a copy of Indian ceremonial chambers where chieftains and elders of each tribe gathered for religious services and powwows. There is one entrance—through the roof—in genuine kivas; for your convenience, a door has been built so you may walk in. Within the kiva the

46

"picture-frame" windows and polished black reflector-mirrors will enchant you. The mirrors' black backgrounds remove the glare but not the color of Canyon and Desert.

Up a flight to the kiva's roof—here is another novelty—upside-down mirrors that show the Canyon and Painted Desert colors in distinct bands. For some reason the colors of the Canyon and Desert stand out in layers or bands if you gaze while standing on your head. This stunt being rather strenuous, the idea of reversed mirrors was invented. Turn your back to the desert, bend over as far as possible, and look at the scenery behind you in this position.

A stairway from the kiva's roof leads to the upper floor of the adjoining watchtower, from which you have one of the most magnificent of Grand Canyon views as well as a sweeping panorama of Kaibab National Forest, the Painted Desert, and the Navajo Indian Country.

While in the Desert View vicinity, you may wish to visit the Trading Post (with soda fountain-luncheonette) that is there. In addition a picnic area, Ranger Station, campground, general store (open during summer only), and service station are to be found here.

The West Rim Drive. Leaving the Visitor Center and Mather Campground headed westward on the Rim Drive, you first pass by the Grand Canyon Village area. Here are located the hospital, general store, bank, post office, community building, public garage, mule barns, laundry, Grand Canyon Auto Cabins and Cafeteria, souvenir shops, Santa Fe Railroad Station, El Tovar Hotel, Bright Angel Lodge and Cabins, and the Hopi House—an authentic reproduction of a Hopi mesa home that houses one of the most complete displays of Indian handicraft in the West. Hopi Indians perform colorful dances on the stone platform near El Tovar Hotel daily at 5:30 P.M. Indoors in cold and stormy weather. (Donations expected.)

Trail View is the first major point of interest along West Rim Drive. Here is a good spot to stop and look at mules and hikers on one of the world's most famous mountain trails. That green spot on the flat plateau (called Tonto Plateau) is Indian Gardens, a popular resting place for trail parties. The building that can be seen is a pump house. Water used at Grand Canyon is lifted from springs in the Inner Canyon at Indian Gardens and Roaring Springs, 3,400 feet below the Rim. Prior to 1932, all water was hauled to Grand Canyon

Miles	Points of Interest	Mile
0.0	Visitor Center, Park Headquarters, and Mather Amphitheater (R). Road to Yavapai Lodge (L)	28.
0.1	Service Station	28.
0.5	Yavapai Point and Museum	28.
1.2	Mather Point parking area	27.
2.0	*Junction.* U.S. 180 and Arizona Route 64. South Entrance Station (1.4 miles); Picnic Area (3.1 miles); and South Park Boundary (4.7 miles)	26.
2.7	Viewpoint	26.
2.9	Viewpoint	26.
3.1	*Junction.* Road to Yaki Point and Head of Kaibab Trail	25.
3.2	Picnic area	25.
4.1	*Junction.* Road to Picnic Area	24.
5.9	Viewpoint	23.
6.7	Viewpoint. Duck on Rock	22.
6.8	Viewpoint	22.
7.9	Picnic Area	21.
8.5	Viewpoint	20.
10.6	*Junction.* Road to Grandview Point	18.
14.0	Picnic area	14.
14.9	Viewpoint	14.
16.6	Viewpoint. Moran Point	12.
18.1	Picnic area	10.
20.5	*Junction.* Road to Wayside Museum and Tusayan Ruin	8.
21.5	Viewpoint	7.
21.8	Viewpoint. Lipan Point	7.
23.0	Viewpoint	5.
23.9	Desert View Point parking area. Watch Tower Visitor Center, Trading Post, and Picnic Area	5.
24.0	*Junction.* Road to District Ranger Station, Desert View Campground and Amphitheater, Service Station	4.
24.1	Desert View Entrance Station	4.
28.9	Park East Boundary	0.

Village by railroad tank car. Water is a scarce and expensive item on *both* Rims, so use it sparingly and wisely.

As noted here, the Tonto Plateau is a wide, flat shelf separating the Inner Gorge from the high walls of the Upper Canyon. Its bench-like nature provides the only natural route of travel through the Canyon. Its relative flatness affords a pleasant rest in the difficult ascent from the River to the Rim. This platform has been cut from a thick layer of very soft rock. Eight hundred feet of hardened mud or shale occur here between the resistant rocks which form the cliff above and below. These shales are readily washed down and eaten

48

back by running water and other elements. The flat Tonto shelf is the result of this erosion.

At Trail View, you are 180 feet higher than El Tovar Hotel (elevation 7,050 feet) because of the Bright Angel Fault. When the great break occurred in the rocks that now form the canyon walls, these rocks on the west side are 180 feet above the corresponding rocks to the east. This can be seen by observing the relative positions of similar strata on the two sides. The break or fault extends across the Grand Canyon and is at least 20 miles long. This example of movement is typical of those which, by elevating the region, made possible the forming of the Grand Canyon. Incidentally, in the deep canyon to the north flows Bright Angel Creek, one of the few permanent tributary streams of the Colorado River in this region. From the rim you cannot see the mouth of Bright Angel Creek, but glimpses may be obtained of its dashing waters at various points higher up. It flows over a rocky bottom of steep declivity and carries a large volume of clear water into the muddy river. In cutting its canyon, this stream has followed the line of the Bright Angel Fault in the rock strata.

Across the Colorado River and slightly to the northwest is a stream bed known as Trinity Creek. Commonly it is completely dry. But its wide valley is an excellent example of the cutting power of running water in this region of little vegetation. Erosion is periodic, due to the aridity of the climate, yet it is none the less effective. Desert plants grow far apart, leaving the slopes partially bare, and the concentrated energy of a single torrential shower here often does more destruction than a season's rainfall on the densely covered slopes of a humid region. The "Shrine of the Ages"—location of summer sunrise religious services—is found at Trail View.

Next stop on your westward journey may be either Maricopa Point (elevation 7,050 feet) or Hopi Point (elevation 7,071 feet). Both are spurs that project from one promontory, and perhaps Hopi gives the wider angle of vision. Both offer spectacular views. You look east, west, north, across miles of buttes and promontories. Those who are interested in identifying the buttes by name can here make out, to the west, the cap of Osiris; to the right of it Dragonhead, Shiva (once part of the North Rim), and Isis; and around to the north Cheops and Buddha. To the east of Bright Angel Canyon are Deva, Brahma, Zoroaster, Walhalla Plateau, and Wotan's Throne; on the

49

far North Rim is Cape Final and in the eastern distance are the Palisades lying in front of the Painted Desert. The high ridge southeast of the Shiva Temple mass consists of Redwall limestone capped by a thick succession of the red Supai rocks. It is tipped by a small remnant of the Coconino sandstone, constituting the striking feature known as Isis Temple. Not long ago geologically, this temple, as well as the closely similar Osiris Temple, was capped by Kaibab limestone as in Buddha, Shiva, and several other of the higher edifices; this has been removed by the elements. Now, having lost the protecting cap of Kaibab limestone, the softer sandstone is being rapidly removed by erosive agencies.

While the view from Hopi and Maricopa Points are excellent for their far vistas, the near portions are less dramatic. You can, however, sight little Horn Creek, the Dana Butte, and great areas of Redwall. The huge rock fragments scattered along the red slopes below have come from the walls of the Canyon. Their breaking-off was due to the combined effects of rain, frost, plant action, temperature changes, and other forces which have been constantly at work cracking and prying off parts of the walls. It is by such ordinary processes of nature, working slowly but steadily, that the great width of the Canyon is accounted for. As the Colorado River has cut its way downward through all of the layers now exposed in the walls, its sides have been constantly breaking down and washing away.

A considerable extent of the Colorado River is seen from Hopi Point. Even though it is several miles away, its muddiness is plainly visible as it flows its swift and tumultuous course. The mighty power of this river, with boulders and sand as its tools, has cut downward through many layers of rock to form the Canyon. Likewise this power has enabled it to carry off the mud, sand, and other materials resulting from excavation. Measurements show that the rate of flow of the River in this section varies between 2½ and 20 miles an hour, and that it averages 300 feet in width and ranges from 10 to 18 feet in depth. The sunsets from Hopi Point are famous. Often, far below you to the west, the brilliant afterglow reflects from the surface of the Colorado River.

Deep shadows of the late afternoon sun are cast over the Canyon. The distant Colorado River, visible lower center, is about 300 feet wide here at Pima Point. Santa Fe Railway photo.

51

On Maricopa Point there is a beautiful memorial to Major John Wesley Powell and his men who first explored the Colorado River through the Grand Canyon in 1869 and again in 1872. This massive monument is constructed of native rock and represents an Aztec sacrificial altar. It was here that the dedication ceremony for Grand Canyon National Park was held on April 30, 1920.

The Rim Road runs west from Maricopa and Hopi Points around by the Inferno (that being the name for the basin or cove due to the red glow of reflected sunset) to Mohave Point. This is another point of observation not too much different from Hopi, though each point at the Canyon has its own variations and possesses certain of its own local features. At Mohave, for instance, your distance view has not materially changed, but you have to the east a fine chance to observe the steep walls of the Kaibab, Toroweap, and Coconino formations under Hopi. Incidentally, the mass of vivid red shales and sandstones just below the point is known as "The Alligator" (this formation is a landmark interesting to geologists because it contains no river gravel indicating that the River has always been approximately where it is now).

The highest cliffs in the Grand Canyon are formed by the Redwall limestone about halfway down. This wall is continuous for many miles in every direction and has an average height of 300 to 400 feet. A brilliant red color characterizes it in most places, but fades into a gray or blue at the ends of promontories where there are no overlying strata. As previously stated in Chapter 2, the red is due to iron oxides which are washed down from the rocks above, staining the face of the wall. The curving and rounded surfaces, amphitheaters, caves, and cavities also characterize the Redwall limestone. These are due to its limy character which allows rain and snow water to reach its surface. Because of its resistance to the breaking and cutting powers of water, wind, and frost, however, it forms massive walls.

On the west side of Mohave Point, there is a small canyon formed by Monument Creek and its upper basin or watershed that is known as the Abyss. The view of the red walls of the Abyss is rather impressive. Also in this canyon stand several isolated rock pillars. The largest is appropriately named The Monument. It is composed of hard brown sandstone. Of similar material are the cliffs forming the canyon walls on each side of it. The unusual hardness of this sandstone enabled it to remain, while rocks about it were worn away. The

Monument represents a last stand against the forces of erosion.

The West Rim Road continues around to Pima. This point (elevation 6,798 feet) is the projecting promontory between Monument and Hermit Creeks. It extends far out into the Canyon and the distance views from it are excellent. To the west are Yuma and Havasupai Points; directly over the mouth of Hermit Creek is Point Sublime; and the various temples and towers of the gods that have been mentioned previously, are to be seen from almost every angle. From Pima Point a large extend of the winding river course, entrenched in the Granite Gorge, is visible. The rocks of this lowest section are upturned and badly shattered. They are the roots of mountains, the upper parts of which were worn away millions of years ago. In these rocks the great alterations of both texture and composition could only have developed under conditions of pressure and heat, requiring an overlying mass of rock many thousands of feet thick. This great covering layer was furnished by the mountains that were washed away.

About 60 miles to the west two dark cone-shaped mountains—Mount Trumbull and Mount Logan—are visible on clear days. Their tops contrast strongly with the flat-topped buttes and mesas so characteristic of this region. The dark color differs from the brilliant red and yellow hues of the surrounding country. These mountains are volcanoes. Molten lavas were forced up through the level plateau surface and in cooling formed these cones.

Something of the power of the Colorado, the force which has enabled it to cut down a mile through layers of hard rock, can be visualized in seeing Monument Rapids from Pima Point. Here the river cascades downgrade at a rate of 20 feet in half a mile. Many of its waves, while they appear as ripples from this distance, are several feet in height. Even from the canyon rim some miles away, the fury of the waves is plainly visible, and at times their roar is audible. This rapids is only one of many in the canyon.

Across the Grand Canyon northwest from Pima Point the level upper surface of the plateau is broken by a single great notch. Careful examination will show that this gap is more than a mere V-shaped cut in the horizontal layers. It is the expression of great movement of those rock layers. To the left, or west, a distinct downward bending is visible, while on the other side the layers, although horizontal, appear to be raised. Thus in this place are seen the results of two movements—a bending, followed by a vertical breaking. One or both of these movements so weakened the surface in that area that the forces of erosion cut the notch.

From Pima Point (named for the Pima Indians of central Arizona), you can see the remnants of old Hermit's Camp and Trail named for the "hermit," who was a miner and prospector living in the basin during the period of the 1880's. The Hermit Trail was used, prior to 1922, by muleback parties for trips to Hermit Camp, a resort that was abandoned when Phantom Ranch was built. All buildings at the resort have been removed to restore the Canyon to its natural state.

At Hermit's Rest, you find a parking area and a rustic stone building with wide porches and large lounge fireplace. This unique cliff-house of Canyon boulders was built in 1914 to provide a resting place for parties using Hermit's Trail, but today it serves as a refreshment and curio shop. The bell at the entrance gate to Hermit's Rest is from an old mission in Guadalajara, Mexico.

From Hermit Rim (elevation 6,700 feet) and in Hermit Basin, just west of Hermit's Rest there are many splendid views. Cope Butte, a long vertical-walled buttress of Redwall, rises steeply to the east; and Marsh Butte, a promontory of closely similar character, projects three miles northwest. On the opposite side of the Inner Gorge and seemingly very near there is a particularly picturesque ridge culminating in the pinnacles known as the Tower of Ra, Osiris Temple, Horus Temple, and the Tower of Set. Farther northwest are Mencius Temple and Confucius Temple, while farther in the distance rises Point Sublime, the great projection at the south end of this portion of the Kaibab Plateau. Just east of Point Sublime is the Hindu Amphitheater, the deep gorge cut through ancient granite rock by Crystal Creek.

There are many "points" jutting out from the south wall of the Canyon west of Hermit Basin, some of which afford superb views of the great chasm and reveal features not visible farther east. Unfortunately, however, these points are some distance from roads and trails and are therefore not convenient to visit. Havasupai Point, Fossil Mountain and Grand Scenic Divide, all near Bass Camp, 25 miles northwest of Grand Canyon Village, have splendid outlooks into a portion of the Canyon full of novelty.

Miles	Points of Interest	Miles

0.0	Visitor Center, Park Headquarters and Amphitheater (R). Road to Yavapai Lodge (L)	8.6
0.1	Road to Camper Service Building, Mather Campground and Grand Canyon Trailer Village	8.5
0.8	Public Service Garage (repairs only)	7.8
0.9	*Junction.* Road to El Tovar Hotel, Hopi House, Verkamp's Store (R). Road to Grand Canyon Village: Fred Harvey Office, Hospital, Bank, General Store, Post Office, Community Building, Stables, Grand Canyon Auto Cabins and Cafeteria, and Village Picnic Area (L)	7.7
1.0	Santa Fe Railroad Station	7.6
1.2	Road to Bright Angel Lodge and Cabins, Kolb Studio, Lookout Photo Studio, and Bright Angel Corral	7.4
1.4	*Junction.* Rowe Well Road (L). Village Picnic Area (0.2 miles), Grand Canyon Auto Cabins and Cafeteria (0.3 miles), Grand Canyon Village (0.4 miles) and South Boundary (3.3 miles). Parking Area for Trail View and Head of Bright Angel Trail (R)	7.2
1.9	Viewpoint	6.7
2.6	Viewpoint	6.0
2.9	Viewpoint	5.7
3.1	*Junction.* Road to Maricopa Point	5.5
3.5	*Junction.* Road to Orphan Mine (not open to public)	5.1
3.7	*Junction.* Road to Hopi Fire Lookout (L) and road to Hopi Point (R)	4.9
3.9	Viewpoint	4.7
4.1	Viewpoint	4.5
4.3	Viewpoint	4.7
4.6	*Junction.* Road to Mohave Point	4.0
4.8	Viewpoint	3.8
5.2	Viewpoint	3.4
5.3	*Junction.* Secondary road to Pasture Wash—leads to start of Havasupai Trail	3.3
5.4	Viewpoint	3.2
5.7	Viewpoint	2.9
6.1	Viewpoint	2.5
6.3	Viewpoint	2.3
6.6	Viewpoint	2.0
7.4	Picnic Area	1.2
7.8	Viewpoint	0.8
7.9	*Junction.* Road to Pima Point	0.7
8.4	Viewpoint	0.2
8.6	Hermit Rest Parking Area	0.0

CONDUCTED MOTOR TRIPS

Motor coaches operated by well-trained driver-guides follow the South Rim's picturesque roads in the following year-round schedule:

Morning Drive to Hermit's Rest (also available as afternoon drive, April 1 to October 31): Motor coaches leave El Tovar Hotel and Bright Angel Lodge, traveling westward over Rim Road along the brink of the chasm. Stops are made at Trail View, Hopi and Pima Points—each offering its own superb view—and finally at Hermit's Rest.

Afternoon Drive to Desert View: After luncheon, motor coaches head from the hotels eastward over East Rim Road. Stops are made at Yavapai Point Museum and at Moran and Lipan Points. The end of the drive eastward brings the traveler to the climax of the trip—the Watchtower at Desert View.

A word to the wise: While on a conducted tour, be ready to hear an occasional tall story. Some of the motor coach drivers delight in entertaining their passengers with some pretty far-out humor. While you are standing on the edge of a thousand foot precipice, for instance, your driver may tell about the lady who fell over the Rim here. She was unhurt because she wore *light fall* clothing! Another tale concerns the man wearing rubber boots—he fell off the Rim here and lit on his feet a thousand feet below. The boots were new and full of bounce—the poor fellow bounced up and down for two days and nights, and a Ranger had to shoot him to keep him from starving to death!

Rather than risk the driver's fun, and yours, we will repeat no more of the old dependables.

Reservation for motor coach tours may be had at the Transportation Desk of either El Tovar Hotel or the Bright Angel Lodge.

SOUTH RIM TRAILS

The *West Rim Trail* follows the edge of the Canyon for a mile and a half from near the corral at Bright Angel Lodge to the Powell Memorial, near Hopi Point. It is an easy and interesting jaunt.

Buses leaving from El Tovar for South Rim drives. Fred Harvey photo.

The *Canyon Rim Nature Trail,* 1½ miles long, leads from El Tovar Hotel to the Visitor Center and the Yavapai Museum. Part of this trail, from the Visitor Center to El Tovar, is self-guiding. (Leaflets are available in dispensers located near El Tovar and the Visitor Center. The numbers along the trail correspond to numbers in this descriptive leaflet.) Try to arrange your arrival at the Yavapai Museum in time for one of the interpretive talks there (see page 35). If you do, you will view the Canyon with much more understanding.

Horseback trips take you through the pine forests, emerging now and then for outstanding views of the Canyon. The trips are available only during the summer, and information on them is available at the Transportation Desk at either El Tovar Hotel or the Bright Angel Lodge.

DRIVING FROM RIM TO RIM

While the Kaibab Trail (the only maintained trail for hikers or riders that connects the two rims) is only 20.6 miles; the trip by motor vehicle is 217! Taking the East Rim Drive, which is Arizona 64, you leave the Park at Desert View and go east to Cameron. Along the way you have several excellent views of Little Colorado River and its gorge.

At Cameron you join U.S. Route 89 and head north into the western portion of the Painted Desert. Here for a distance of 20 miles you will see Shadow Mountain on the western horizon, always appearing draped in shadows at its summit. The mountain has long been a landmark in this land which held many terrors for early travelers.

Passing through the Painted Desert you approach the foothills, spotted with junipers (wrongly called cedars by many). Soon you will see the scattered Navajo earth-covered lodges called hogans. You may also see the Indians themselves, tending the small bands of sheep grazing along the washes and arroyos. Particularly in July and August the Navajos—since most of their activities are out-of-doors—may easily be viewed by the traveler. Along the roadside you may even note small fields of Indian corn on each of the sandy bars of the washes (dry creek beds that at certain seasons carry a large volume of water).

Looking toward the South Rim from Point Sublime on the North Rim. Union Pacific Railroad photo.

In the midst of this fascinating land you will come upon a couple of trading posts—The Gap (with very inviting accommodations for meals and lodging) and Cedar Ridge where the Navajos gather around the post. A short or extended stop at either of the trading posts will be rewarding.

Progressing toward Marble Canyon of the Colorado, Echo Cliffs come into view. One good shout, and the returning echo will tell you that these cliffs are properly named. After swinging onto U.S. Route 89A, you approach Navajo Bridge spanning Marble Canyon, which in a real sense linked together the state of Arizona, replacing the old Lee's Ferry and the Colorado "dug-way." After crossing this high, narrow suspension-bridge you will want to stop at the parking area and look down into this infant canyon of the Grand Canyon of the Colorado, which you will see later from points on the North Rim. Incidentally, the Navajo Bridge is the only one (except for the Kaibab Bridge across the Inner Canyon) between Moab, Utah, and Lake Mead, or for a distance of about a thousand miles.

Continuing along past the beautiful Vermilion Cliffs you move toward pastoral House Rock Valley where on a Federal Refuge a herd of about 200 buffalo often shares the range with many head of Hereford cattle. You may be able to see some of the buffalo, but at times they drift far from the area traversed by the highway.

From House Rock Valley you ascend through the junipers and pinons to the Kaibab Plateau. Soon you are at Jacob Lake and Arizona Route 67 beckons you southward into the very heart of Kaibab National Forest and to the North Rim of the Grand Canyon.

GETTING TO KNOW THE NORTH RIM

The high Kaibab Plateau north of Grand Canyon is cool and moist, in contrast with the desert encircling it below. Kaibab is a Paiute Indian word meaning "mountain-lying-down," a description that fits it well, particularly when seen from a distance. This vast plateau, some 50 miles long and 35 miles wide, is isolated on the south and east by the Grand Canyon, on the north and west by the wide plains, above which it rises 5,000 feet. In elevation it stands from 7,500 to 9,300 feet above sea level. This means that North Rim has a cooler climate, different plant life, and offers an entirely different type of view. Many of the familiar formations rising out of the "great deep"—such as

Wotan's Throne, Angel's Gate, Mount Hayden, and the Temples of Shiva, Zoroaster, Deva, and Brahma—are closer to the North Rim, and a much closer view may be obtained from there. The many observation points on the North Rim afford a superb view of the Painted Desert and all the colorful regions extending back to the volcanic peaks of the San Francisco Range.

NORTH RIM ROADS

There are two main roads on the North Rim; one leads to Bright Angel Point, the other to Cape Royal out on the huge Walhalla Plateau (locally called "Greenland"). Incidentally, the Walhalla Plateau, which is across Bright Angel Canyon from Bright Angel Point, was the home of early Indians. Items found here indicate that they lived in this area from 700 A.D. to 1175 and then left suddenly leaving all behind.

The North Entrance Road: Before reaching the northern boundary of Grand Canyon National Park, Arizona Route 67, from Jacobs Lake, takes you through a portion of Kaibab National Forest. There Nature has somehow achieved that cleanness of pattern that permits you to look down long aisles of ponderosa pine, Douglas-fir and Engelmann spruce. But the Kaibab also has its "parks," open, grassy meadows, fringed with aspens that in autumn turn to a rich golden glow.

The witchery of these sylvan meadows is wholly irresistible; they seem designed for parades and pageants, for the lighthearted moods of man and beast. And so, indeed, they are employed. Afternoon and morning they are the gathering places of many of the herds of blacktail mule deer that range unfrightened through the forest, which was once a noted Indian hunting ground. Another interesting Kaibab creature is the white-tailed Kaibab squirrel (*Sciurus kaibabensis*), which may ordinarily be seen flickering through the forest near Jacobs Lake Ranger Station. This is the most beautiful squirrel in the Western Hemisphere, and one of the rarest, for it lives *nowhere* else. It is about the size of a large gray squirrel, though shorter and stockier, is dark bluish-gray marked with brown, has long tufted ears and a broad feathery tail that is almost pure white. The Kaibab squirrel is, however, one of the shyest of the Kaibab's inhabitants, almost impos-

sible to approach close enough to photograph, flashing through the trees of the Kaibab like a white comet.

A short distance past the entrance checking station, you will find a primitive secondary dirt road that leads to Point Sublime some 16.6 miles away. This point, at an elevation of 7,464 feet, affords a spectacular 150-mile view from east to west. Here the Inner Canyon seems to come closer than at any other spot along the North Rim. Actually, this promontory extends almost 10 miles out into the canyon between huge basins that lie more than 3,000 feet below. The huge point visible on the South Rim is Havasupai Point. Point Sublime was named by Major Clarence E. Dutton when he described it in 1880 as "by far the most sublime of the earthly spectacles." Before undertaking the drive check with the ranger at entrance station as to the road's condition, since in wet weather it may be impassable, while in dry weather, it may be closed because of forest-fire danger.

After passing the entrance station, the main road passes through old Robbers Roost Canyon. This area was made popular in two of Zane Grey's books—*Man of the Forest* and *Robbers Roost*. Robbers Roost Canyon is so named, according to local stories, because in a bygone time, this portion of Kaibab was used as a hideout for a gang of thieves.

Once past Robbers Roost Canyon, you go over Lindberg Hill, into Thompson Canyon, and then by the North Rim village area— the District Ranger Station, grocery store, gas station, gift shop, garage, Bright Angel Campground and North Rim Inn. The road finally ends at the Grand Canyon Lodge on Bright Angel Point.

The Grand Canyon Lodge and Bright Angel Point are located at the head of Bright Angel Canyon, where a most spectacular view of the canyon may be enjoyed. The Lodge is built right on the canyon rim, where large open verandas and massive windows afford an intimate view of the temples and buttes below. A Park Naturalist conducts an interesting program each evening in the recreation room of the Lodge as well as at the North Rim Campground Amphitheater.

As you stand on lofty Bright Angel Point (elevation 8,153 feet), Roaring Spring Canyon is on your left and The Transept is the Can-

---

Angels Window, a hole through a thin point of rock projecting into the Canyon near Cape Royal, is familiar to North Rim visitors. (Lower right-hand corner of picture) Union Pacific Railroad photo.

yon to the right. Erosion continues to eat away at the ridge; Bright Angel Point might someday be isolated from the rim to become a temple or butte. By the way, those three peaks that you see so clearly are Deva Temple, Brahma Temple, and Zoroaster Temple. (This view of the three temples appeared on a 2¢ postage stamp issued in 1934.) Because the South Rim is about 1,200 feet lower than the North Rim, you can see the vast Coconino Plateau, while the mountains on the skyline are the San Francisco Peaks, 60 air-miles away, and just north of Flagstaff, Arizona. The highest is Humphreys Peak, Arizona's tallest mountain, towering to 12,670 feet. These were active volcanoes at three different periods during the last one million years. Sunset Crater, a National Monument 14 miles north of Flagstaff, is a volcano that erupted in 1064 A.D.—just over 900 years ago. Surrounding the bases of the San Francisco Mountains are lava flows that extend for many miles. Grand Canyon National Park itself, however, is remarkably free from "recent-day" volcanic material, yet here, close by, is one of the largest volcanic areas in the United States. Much closer at hand than the mountains and almost directly ahead is the protuberance called Red Butte, the only visible remains of the whole Mesozoic Era.

As you stand on Bright Angel Point, you may wonder why the South Rim is lower than the North Rim. This is because when the river cut through the original dome-shaped plateau (see page 20) it cut about 10 miles south of the highest part (the North Rim). The Colorado River cannot be seen from Bright Angel Point, due to the fact that it is so much farther from the North Rim to the River than from the South Rim to the River. On the South Rim the drainage is away from the Canyon but on the North Rim it is into the Canyon. Therefore, the water from rain and snow has cut back the north side much farther from the river. Also there is more precipitation on the North Rim.

Precipitation in this area averages about 29 inches a year. Part of this comes in the winter as snow (which ranges around 200 inches in depth) and the balance as summer thunderstorms—usually during August.

Cape Royal Road: This road has the widest variety of scenery in the Park. After leaving the junction with the North Entrance Road, you ride through beautifully wooded areas as well as open alpine meadows. Chances are good that you may see a deer near the road, or even a

Miles	Points of Interest	Miles
0.0	North Park Boundary	12.9
0.2	Entrance Station	12.7
0.7	*Junction*. Road to Point Sublime (16.6 miles)	12.2
10.0	*Junction*. Cape Royal Road	2.9
10.1	*Trail head*. Kaibab Trail	2.8
11.7	*Junction*. Road to Ranger Station (0.1 mile). Information service and exhibit room	1.2
11.9	*Junction*. Road to Gas Station (0.1 mile); Grocery Store and Gift Shop (0.2 mile); North Rim Inn and Bright Angel (North Rim) Campground (0.3 mile)	1.0
12.1	*Junction*. Road to Public Service Garage—repair work only (0.1 mile), Service Road to mule and horse stables (0.3 mile)	0.8
12.7	Bright Angel Point viewpoint parking area. Start of Bright Angel Point self-guiding nature trail	0.2
12.9	Grand Canyon Lodge	0.0

Kaibab squirrel, especially in early morning or evening. There are several turnouts where you can stop to view the woodland scenery.

When you reach the junction with the road to Point Imperial, either turn now, or make a mental note to do it on your return from Cape Royal. At Point Imperial, with Saddle Mountain to your left and Mount Hayden rising out of the canyon at your feet, you can again gaze down upon the lower plateau of the South Rim, but this time if you look to the east, Painted Desert and Echo Cliffs can be seen. The line of the Vermilion Cliffs may be seen extending to the solitary cone of Navajo Mountain, 90 miles to the northeast. This is the highest point (8,801 feet) along either rim of the Grand Canyon and thus has been called "imperial."

On the road to Cape Royal, you will come to Greenland Lake overlook. This lake is rare indeed for there are no streams on either rim. The upper rock formations in the Canyon are porous and water finds its way down through the strata until it reaches a rock layer it cannot pass through. The water travels along on top of this impervious layer, downslope, dissolving out channels or caverns, until it comes out in the Canyon wall as a "spring." (Roaring Springs and the springs at Indian Garden are fine examples of this.) But, on the Kaibab and Walhalla Plateaus and through the meadows the roofs of many channels and caverns have collapsed forming sinkholes. The absence of streams is accounted for by all drainage going into sinks (referred to as interior drainage). An area having many sinkholes is called "a karst region," or an area of Karst topography. Occasionally a sink becomes plugged with mud and vegetation and becomes a pond or a lake as water drains in. This is what happened here at Greenland Lake. Incidentally, all the water that you use on the North Rim is pumped up 3,460 feet from Roaring Springs.

The next major viewpoint along the Cape Royal road is Farview Point (elevation 8,300 feet). Here a wide view of the Painted Desert stretches out to the eastward, and the smoke from the powerhouse at Tuba City can usually be seen. To the north, the mountains of Utah are plainly visible.

As you continue along, several other viewpoints offer opportunities to see the eastern portion of the Canyon and lands beyond. At Angel's Window, you are able to witness a large hole that has been eroded through a spur of Kaibab limestone which projects into the Canyon. A short footpath leads from Cape Royal to the top of the "Window," which is several hundred feet below the rim.

Cape Royal, itself, is in one of the widest parts of the Grand Canyon, with the South Rim 10 to 12 miles away and the river over a mile below. In addition to being able to obtain glimpses of the river, you can view Wotan's Throne and Vishnu Temple most clearly. Ranger talks are given daily here on the Grand Canyon's geology. Picnic tables, rest rooms and two primitive campsites are also available at the Cape.

Miles	Points of Interest	Miles
0.0	*Junction*. North Entrance Road	20.1
1.6	Turnout. Interesting forest-meadow area. Deer often may be seen here	18.5
3.9	Picnic Area	16.2
5.3	Turnout	14.8
5.5	*Junction*. Road to Point Imperial (2.8 miles)	14.6
8.1	Greenland Lake Overlook	12.0
10.2	Viewpoint and Picnic Area. Vista Encantada (Enchanting view)	9.9
12.0	Viewpoint. Farview Point	8.1
14.2	Turnout	5.9
18.6	Viewpoint. Cape Final	1.5
19.6	Viewpoint. Angel's Window	0.5
20.1	Cape Royal Parking Area	0.0

CONDUCTED MOTOR TRIP

There is a daily afternoon bus trip from Grand Canyon Lodge to Point Imperial and Cape Royal. Information on this junket, which includes a nature talk at Cape Royal, may be obtained from the Transportation Desk at the Lodge.

NORTH RIM TRAILS

The *Bright Angel Point Rim Walk* starts at the Kaibab Trail Head Parking Area and proceeds to Bright Angel Point at Grand Canyon Lodge. The last quarter-mile of this 2.1 mile trail is a self-guiding *Nature Trail*. This Nature Trail starts at the trail shelter at Bright Angel Point parking area and proceeds to the Point. Leaflets are available at the shelter and at a dispenser below Grand Canyon Lodge. The numbers along the trail correspond to numbers in this leaflet.

The *Transept Canyon Path* is an interesting and leisurely 1.6-mile trail that meanders along the rim of the Canyon between Grand Canyon Lodge and Bright Angel (North Rim) Campground. Near the bottom of Transept Canyon is a vertical Redwall cliff, 550 feet high. Here, as is visible from the trail, water has dissolved many caverns and caves within this nearly pure limestone and dolomite formation. It was in these caves that early evidence of the existence of man at Grand Canyon was found—figurines, three to ten inches in height, made of split twigs. Their purpose is unknown, but perhaps prehistoric hunters placed them in the caves to insure a successful hunt.

At *Cape Royal,* a half-mile self-guiding Nature Trail with points-of-interest signs starts at the Cape Royal Parking Area and leads you to the tip of Cape Royal.

While these are the only *maintained* rim trails, several others will take you through great open forests of the region. The major ones are:

Name	Termini	Length in Miles
Walhalla Plateau Trail	Cape Royal Road (near turn-out at 14.2 mile point) to Rim	14.0
Obi Point Trail	Cape Royal Road (near Vista Encantadora Viewpoint) to Obi Point	6.4
Sublime Meadows Trail	Loop of Point Sublime Road	6.0
Walla Valley Trail	Point Sublime to Rim	3.0
Upper Bright Angel Canyon Trail	Cape Royal Road (near turnout at 1.6 mile point) to upper point of Kaibab Trail	6.7
Natchi Point Trail	North Entrance Road (Kaibab Trail parking area) to Natchi Point	3.4

Horseback trips leave daily, in morning and afternoon, from the stables near CCC Hill and follow the Natchi Point Trail to Uncle Jim Point.* Special parties can be arranged to make horse trips to such spots as Oza Butte and Thunder River. The latter is a five-day pack trip usually made only in late spring and early fall. Make reservations for all horse trips with Jack Church & Sons, Inc., P.O. Box 370, Kanab, Utah 84741, or at the Transportation Desk at the Grand Canyon Lodge.

GRAND CANYON NATIONAL MONUMENT

Grand Canyon National Monument, described on pages 161-168, may be approached from U.S. Route 89A at Fredonia, Arizona; State Routes 59 and 389 at Colorado City (formerly Short Creek), Arizona; and U.S. Route 91 at St. George, Utah. (From Fredonia, the Monument is 65 miles; from Colorado City—55 miles; and St. George—90 miles.) Sections of the route from St. George are often impassable

* Uncle Jim Owens was a pioneer who settled near here and was a friend and guide for President Theodore Roosevelt when he visited the Grand Canyon in 1914.

From Toroweap Overlook, a cliff plunges 3,000 feet to the Colorado River in the Grand Canyon National Monument. National Park Service photo.

from October to May due to heavy snows on Mount Trumbull. Regardless of the direction of approach, Mount Trumbull, at the head of the Toroweap Valley, is an excellent reference point along the poorly signed roads. While none of these routes is improved, they are graded and kept in generally fair condition. They may become impassable for short periods following heavy storms.

After leaving Colorado City or Fredonia, there is no habitation until you arrive at the Tuweep Ranger Station. For this reason, it is inadvisable for anyone to attempt the trip without ample gasoline, water, food, camp outfit, and tools. Limited water is available at the Tuweep Ranger Station, where a National Park Service ranger is on duty the year round. There are no lodging or meal accommodations available. A small campground is located south of the ranger station near the Rim.

After passing the ranger station, the road leads on 6 miles to the brink of Grand Canyon, where one obtains a view entirely different from anywhere else. Here the Canyon averages less than a mile in width and nearly 3,000 feet in depth, to produce a really breathtaking spectacle. The roar of Lava Falls Rapids is clearly audible on quiet days. A trip into this area, one of the most remote in Northern Arizona, should not be attempted without adequate preparation and equipment.

PIPE SPRING NATIONAL MONUMENT

On your way from Fredonia to Grand Canyon National Monument, you will pass near Pipe Spring National Monument. This picturesque, well-preserved Mormon fort at Pipe Spring evidences the need felt by the pioneers to protect themselves from the native Indian tribes. Much credit is due the Mormons, who settled at Pipe Spring and many other places in the region, for the exploration, colonization, and development of this part of the Southwest. Under the leadership of Brigham Young, they established their religion and way of life in this formidable land. As an expression of the courage, foresight, and faith of our pioneers in general, and the Mormons in particular, Pipe Spring is an especially appropriate monument.

While in the Grand Canyon area, the Mormon fort at Pipe Spring National Monument is a worthwhile visit. National Park Service photo.

71

Members of the Jacob Hamblin party, the first white men to visit Pipe Spring, camped at this spring in 1858. They had been sent out by Brigham Young to explore and report on the Colorado River country and to negotiate, if possible, a treaty of peace with the Navajos living on the south side of the river.

William Hamblin (Gunlock Bill), a member of the party, was considered one of the best rifle shots in the Southwest. While camping at the spring, some of the men tricked him into trying to shoot through a silk handkerchief at 50 paces. He failed in the attempt, because the handkerchief, hung by the upper edge only, yielded before the force of the bullet. Somewhat vexed, he dared one of the men to put his pipe on a rock near the spring, which was at some distance, so that the mouth of the bowl faced directly toward them. He then wagered that he could shoot the bottom out of the bowl without touching the rim. The wager accepted, "Gunlock Bill" promptly and neatly performed the feat and won the wager—hence the name Pipe Spring.

Dr. James M. Whitmore and Robert McIntyre first settled Pipe Spring in 1863 as a cattle ranch. They built a dugout of juniper logs and earth to use as their headquarters. Both men were massacred by a band of marauding Navajos and Paiutes during the winter of 1865-66.

The Mormons, under the direction of Brigham Young, acquired the Whitmore-McIntyre estate; and, in 1869, Bishop Anson P. Winsor arrived at Pipe Spring to build a fort, improve the spring, and take care of the cattle tithed for the church. By 1871, he had finished the fort, which was called by some "Winsor Castle." Nestled near the base of the colorful Vermilion Cliffs, it consisted of two two-story red sandstone buildings. They faced each other across a courtyard which was closed at the ends with a high sandstone wall and heavy gates. There was a firing platform a few feet below the top of one wall, and several loopholes can now be observed that could have been used in case of Indian attack.

Guide service is provided daily from 8 A.M. to 5 P.M. You are requested to picnic only in the designated area. The superintendent of Zion National Park is in charge of the monument. Communications should be addressed to him at Springdale, Utah 84767, or to the Acting Superintendent, Pipe Spring National Monument, Moccasin Rural Station, Fredonia, Arizona 86022.

PHOTOGRAPHY IN THE PARK

Photography has an irresistible appeal to visitors of Grand Canyon National Park. In this land of color, a camera is indispensable.

South Rim. Just about any time is good for taking pictures on the South Rim except from 10 A.M. until 2 P.M. when the light is flat—then you will need shadows or clouds to give definition to Canyon formations. The period from midafternoon until sunset is best for color photography because the Canyon colors then are most vivid. Early morning is good after the sun is high enough to strike into the Canyon; the air then is clear and there is little dust. During the summer months, a sunset photography walk is given along the canyon rim from Yavapai Museum to Grandeur Point (a quarter-mile). On this walk, which starts about 7 P.M. to about 15 minutes after sunset, advice is given on taking sunset Canyon shots.

Use filters for both black-and-white and color film, especially if the air is hazy. For panoramic views, stop down your lens and shoot more slowly—nothing is moving out there! Summer brings thunderheads for dramatic pictures and sparkling air for good visibility as soon as the storms have ended.

Both Kolb and Lookout Studios, near the Bright Angel Lodge, will help you with photographic problems; either will have your film processed.

North Rim. As on the South Rim, best hours for taking pictures are before 10 A.M. and after 2 P.M. For panoramas, set up a tripod at any of three major lookout points—Royal, Imperial, or Sublime. For sunsets, try Vista Encantada because the sunsets do strange and wonderful things to the desert, which will be the background for your pictures.

If you are on the Rim in the autumn, you should note that the light is not as strong as it is in the summer, so take careful meter readings, especially for color. Give the aspens plenty of exposure, and try some of them in black-and-white, with a heavy yellow filter. Wait for some fluffy clouds to appear in that blue sky, and you will have a picture to remember.

Chapter 4.

Exploring the Canyon

T HE best way *really* to see and *fully* appreciate the Grand Canyon is to go down into it. Any able-bodied person of almost any age can make the trip. You will return with a sense of new dimensions of beauty, size, and grandeur. This is a soul-satisfying experience. No roads lead into and down the Canyon—only trails. The trip down and back demands muscle and fiber—the experience is unforgettable.

MULE TRIPS INTO THE CANYON

Going by muleback is the easiest way to see the Colorado River and view the Canyon from within. Mule trips may be taken from either Rim, and they, as well as the Phantom Ranch in the Inner Canyon, are operated by concessioners under contract with the Government.

Suitable riding clothes—slacks, or dungarees—and a broad-brimmed hat are required for all mule trips. (On the South Rim, apparel of this type may be rented at El Tovar Hotel or the Bright Angel Lodge.) In winter, warm clothes are necessary. But remember that only items that can fit into a 2 × 6 × 8-inch space, plus a small camera (no tripod), can be carried. Water and lunch are provided on mule Canyon trips.

Persons weighing over 200 pounds (fully clothed), children under twelve years of age, or pets, cannot be taken on mule trips. No regular facilities are provided, but it may be possible for you to make arrangements with local residents for care of your children or pets while you are on trail trips. The desk clerk at one of the lodges or at your

Late afternoon finds a mule trail party returning on the Bright Angel Trail to the South Rim. Santa Fe Railway photo.

hotel will have a list of baby- or pet-sitters available in Grand Canyon Village.

Grand Canyon's "long-eared taxis" are about the safest transportation known. This fact should reassure the visitor who has clambered aboard a mule in the little round corral at the trail-head, all full of bravado and adventure, and then suddenly is expected to ride off the Rim of all visible creation. That little ledge of trail seems awfully narrow; frequently the rider may hesitate for as much as a couple of minutes.

About 60 to 65 mules are used each day on the South Rim trips. Under the handling of very competent guides, they are gentle and well-seasoned. Many of the mules have been in service for over twenty years. New mules from four to six years of age are purchased regularly in Kansas or Missouri. Their weight must be between 900 and 1400 pounds. Preferably, unbroken stock is chosen. Those selected are shipped to Grand Canyon and their education begins. They are often reluctant and indifferent students, but generally the guile and patience of the instructors outlasts the immobility of the mule.

First, of course, comes a period for the mule to get used to the altitude. This takes about a week and is very important, as otherwise a mule's wind would be poor. Meanwhile, he is taught to lead, to go into the barn for his feed, and that his two-legged rider in overalls and a big hat is a good guy to get along with up to a certain point.

Early-day training requires a period of service in the pack string that daily plods from Yaki Point down the South Kaibab Trail to Phantom Ranch with gasoline, hay, groceries, mail, laundry, and the stack of other items needed there. But the trail guides believe that the way to teach a mule to carry a rider is to ride him, and that's the training he gets now. He is ridden around the corral; he is ridden out through the woods. He may be ridden over for his first view of his future workroom—the Grand Canyon and its trails.

Kickers and buckers among the new mules receive special attention. Modern treatment for kicking calls for hitching an old automobile tire to a leg by a short hobble for twenty-four hours or whatever longer time it takes for the mule to learn that the tire comes back and harmlessly whacks him again every time he tries to kick it off toward the North Rim. This tire, passed around from foot to foot until the mule

---

A mule party rides along the River Trail above the Colorado River. Fred Harvey photo.

treats it with full contempt, does the job. From then on—confronted by rocks, papers, raincoats—he will not budge. Or, if he bucks, the same tire hitched to the saddle horn by about a foot of good rope will soon solve the problem. Every time the mule jumps, the tire jerks around and whacks him on the neck, the sides, or the back. He soon gives up with great disgust at himself for being such a fool as to fight it. But most mules never buck and never need this treatment. They serve a training period as mounts for the guides; and if still tractable and patient, in two or three months may be started out with a tourist rider aboard.

This is the crucial test. Some mules never pass it. But, if a mule has not been abused, and if he feels confidence in man generally, within a week from his graduation he finds that he is boss of the whole outfit. The rider on his back is usually hanging onto everything but the reins, and he—the mule—can go right on doing the few things he has learned. The world is full of hay and oats every evening, and occasional bites of sugar and ham sandwiches, and lots of love and affection from his rider.

While his training has been going on, the guides have been thinking up a name for him. Some mules are named for guides or those they wish to honor. Others for guides' girl friends. Mainly, however, they are named for some peculiarity of their own.

The guides, of course, have quite a line of conversation that goes with the mule trip. One of the most common questions at the head of the trail, the foreman reports is, "Have you a real gentle mule for me?" To this the guide is likely to reply solemnly, "No ma'am, I'm right sorry, but we just sent the last gentle mule down with the last party. If you ain't ever rode before, why we'll just give you a mule that ain't ever been rode before either, an' you can start right out together."

Another common bit of advice the guide may hand out deals with hanging on. "Just you hang right onto that saddle horn, lady," he will advise the frightened female from Boston. "Just you hang right onto it, an' pull hard. If you pull it off, just hand it to me an' I'll put it back on for you."

Or the advice may be—"If you fall off, be sure you keep your eyes open for they tell me the scenery's awful purty on the way down!" This lightness of attitude usually relaxes the novice passengers and they start out expecting to have a good trip. At the end of the day after they get back to the Rim most of them will admit that it *was* a good trip.

There are three basic mule trips that leave the South Rim and go down into the Canyon daily. The one-day *Plateau Point Trip* is an all-year junket that follows the Bright Angel Trail (see below) and takes about 7½ hours. It is perhaps the oldest trail at the Canyon. The bighorn sheep and the Indians followed it many years before the coming of the white man, trappers and explorers used it before Powell, and when copper was discovered in the Canyon a mining company took it over and made it negotiable by burros freighted with packs of copper. It was copper that built most of the railway up from Williams in connection with the trail, and when the mine failed, it was the Santa Fe that took over the railway, completed it, built El Tovar at the end of the line, and opened the Canyon to more tourists —even down to the River and beyond.

The trail starts west of the Bright Angel Lodge and descends Jacob's Ladder, a set of switchbacks through the Redwall. It emerges on a sloping spread of shale, the Tonto Plateau. Into these shales a valley has been excavated, without man's help, to hold the miraculous green of Indian Gardens. Cottonwood trees offer welcome shade. Garden Creek, which proceeds from it, is bordered for a way with willow, grape, arrowweed, and redbud. Indians once used the bubbling springs to irrigate small fields. When early prospectors came, there were still patches of beans and squash, planted by the Havasupais. The trail party usually makes this the lunch stop, relaxing at picnic tables in a bright oasis. After the stop, the mules take you to the north edge of the Tonto Rim to Plateau Point for a view straight down into the Inner Gorge that falls 1,380 feet to the river. Up- and down-Canyon, nothing but crystal-sharp air stands between the spectator and massive buttes and mesas, lifting their colored walls, side gorges breaking away in the marvelous complexities of the Grand Canyon System. Return to the South Rim is made over the same route.

The one-day *Colorado River Trip* takes about 8½ hours, but it is discontinued from November 1 to March 1. It follows the Bright Angel Trail to Indian Gardens and Plateau Point, then turns northeast, down into the Valley of Pipe Creek, twists through the Devil's Corkscrew in more switchbacks and approaches the river. At the river's edge, called by the Havasu Indians, "The Place of the Roaring Sound," where the Bright Angel Trail ends, the trip reaches the halfway mark and turns back (after lunch), on the same trail. Pictures of each trail party are taken as the party starts down and they may be purchased at the Kolb Studio.

The two-day *Phantom Ranch Trip* is a journey to a guest ranch in the bottom of Grand Canyon. It is available year round. This trip follows the Bright Angel Trail to its end, and then goes along the River Trail (see page 17) to the Kaibab Suspension Bridge, which is 440 feet long, 5 feet wide, and 60 feet above the river. A long tunnel of solid granite was blasted through to make the approach, and the bridge is securely anchored and slung with steel cables high over the water. (The nearest highway bridge is 131 miles northeast and it crosses the Colorado at the head of Marble Canyon.) A mile or so beyond the bridge, the trail, now the Northern Section of the Kaibab (see page 81), enters Bright Angel Canyon and then goes on to Phantom Ranch, as remote and delightful a little paradise as any traveler could hope for. Under big cottonwoods, rustic cabins of wood and stone, recreation hall, and dining hall are clustered around a turquoise swimming pool. There is comfort indeed for pleasantly tired muscles, excellent food for the ravenous appetite, and friendly companionship. You can listen in on the after-dinner talk of the guides and packers—usually about the all-important mules, those kings of the trail.

In 1903, David Rust established, near Phantom Creek, a camp for travelers and hunting parties, calling it Rust's Camp. Four years later he put in a cable sixty feet above the stream across the Colorado. Rust's tramway furnished a safe way to cross the turbulent river. In 1913, the location was referred to as Roosevelt's Camp because Theodore Roosevelt stayed there. In 1921, the present resort was constructed at the Old Rust Camp by Fred Harvey. Phantom Ranch was named after Phantom Canyon—so named by the early surveyors because of the illusory effect of the narrow gorge as seen from above in the late afternoon.

After a pleasant night's rest, the next morning the mule party returns to South Rim via the Southern Section of Kaibab Trail. The trip up is usually somewhat faster than the trip down, so the party returns to Yaki Point in time for lunch. For those who wish, extra days may be spent at Phantom Ranch by special arrangement with Fred Harvey (see page 169).

A cross-Canyon trip may be arranged during the summer for parties of three or more. This trip leads down to Phantom Ranch and

80

Phantom Ranch is the overnight stop for trail parties spending more than a day on the trail. Santa Fe Railway photo.

on northward through Bright Angel Canyon, past picturesque Ribbon Falls and Roaring Springs, to the North Rim. Return may be made by either mule over Kaibab Trail or by a 217-mile auto trip or by airplane (see page 183).

For mule trips into the Canyon from the South Rim, confirmed reservations should be made as far in advance as possible with Fred Harvey Transportation, Grand Canyon, Arizona 86023, or with the firm's offices in Chicago and Los Angeles (see page 169). Arrangements for these trips may be made at the transportation desks at El Tovar Hotel or the Bright Angel Lodge.

NORTH RIM MULE TRIPS

There is only one regularly scheduled daily trip from the North Rim. This is the 8½-hour trip to Roaring Springs and return. It follows the Northern Section of Kaibab to Roaring Springs Fall, where the lunch stop is made. These springs at the head of Bright Angel Creek gush with such force from the canyon wall that the result is a true roaring sound. The water then plunges 400 feet down a fern-covered slope. Along the trail are frequent views of Manzanita Canyon and of the eastern wall of Bright Angel Canyon about four miles away. The water pipe, visible at intervals along the trail, carries water pumped from Bright Angel Creek to the North Rim. (Roaring Springs also supplies some of the water to the South Rim by means of a transcanyon pipeline.) The steep walls of Manzanita Canyon are descended in switchbacks along the Redwall, which is nearly perpendicular. A three-quarter mile tunnel has been blasted from the solid limestone. The open side affords views of the Canyon and a pretty little creek. Bright Angel Creek, by the way, was so named by Major Powell after he made the trip through the Canyon in 1869: Clear water was very scarce on the voyage so when this clear, cold stream was reached the explorer was so elated that he named it the Bright Angel.

A two-day trip is available that takes you all the way to Phantom Ranch. (A minimum of three persons is required for this trip.) When you leave the Bright Angel Point area on the mule trip to Phantom Ranch, the trail is in deep shade. Then suddenly you descend into the canyon on a trail that in places has been cut out of solid rock.

Ribbon Falls as seen from the North Kaibab Trail. Fred Harvey photo.

Roaring Springs, just below Bright Angel Point, is your first stop. At Cottonwood Camp, halfway between Roaring Springs and Ribbon Falls, you will find that the temperature has risen some 30° since you left Bright Angel Point, for you have dropped almost 4,000 feet, plus it is also later in the day. At Ribbon Falls, 9 miles along on your 14-mile journey to the river, you will want to stop for the scenery. The last 5 miles will be the hottest, but they will be shady, and soon you will reach Phantom Ranch. You will have made a trip which, in terms of changing climate, is like going from Canada to Mexico.

Make reservations for all North Rim trips with Jack Church & Sons, Inc., P.O. Box 370, Kanab, Utah 84741.

INNER CANYON HIKING

Going on foot can be rugged. Unless you are very certain of your stamina, do not attempt to hike to the river. A canyon trip is the reverse of mountain climbing. The uphill grind comes at the end, not at the beginning when you are fresh. The climb out means an ascent of nearly 5,000 feet. However, for those able to stand this exertion, a hiking trip into Grand Canyon well repays the effort. It is a fine way to realize a greater appreciation of the size of the Canyon and the magnificence of Inner Canyon scenery. A few commercial operators offer guided hiking trips through the Canyon and a list of their names will be sent on request from the Superintendent's office (see page 10).

Only the Bright Angel and Kaibab Trails are presently maintained by the National Park Service. Most of the others are old mining trails that have not been used or maintained in the past fifty years. Time and extensive rock slides have obliterated parts of *all* the old trails, and a topographic map (see page 185) and ability to use it are prerequisites to any travel along these routes. Do not gauge your endurance, time, water requirements, or ability to find the way by previous hiking experience. Veteran hikers of the Sierras, Rockies, and Alps attest to the fact that Grand Canyon hiking is a totally different situation. No one should venture down any of the old trails without first checking with a Park Ranger and traveling a similar distance on one of the used, maintained trails, the Bright Angel or the Kaibab.

Summer Inner Canyon temperatures, sometimes as high as 125°, plus exertion, normally reduce a man's efficiency to one-half. Know

Roaring Springs, with Uncle Jim Point in the background, is the source of much of the water used on both Rims. Union Pacific Railroad photo.

the symptoms of dehydration, heat exhaustion, sunstroke, and be prepared to cope with them. Shade, rest, water, and conservation of sweat can partly offset the lesser ill effects of extreme heat. When possible, travel at the cooler times of day, resting in shade during midday heat. Do not expose your skin to the sun but wear a thin covering of light-colored clothes plus a light hat. Salt tablets are not necessary. Your body can partially adjust to lack of salt but not to lack of fluids. Your life is dependent on the water you carry. During high summer heat it is recommended that each hiker start out with no less than *one-half gallon* of water for descending into the Canyon, and *one gallon* per day for consumption while ascending any trail. Emergency mule service is available for those hikers too exhausted to walk out of the Canyon. However, it is expensive, and the need for it is avoidable if hikers take proper precautions and do not over-estimate their hiking abilities.

The tendency on a first hike in unfamiliar terrain is to overload your pack. Water should be the heaviest single item. In summer a blanket is sufficient for cover while sleeping. Food for a two-day hike should not include too many extras. Remember, dehydrated food can be used only where there is a known water supply. Canned foods are heavy but probably necessary. Snack often along the way, particularly on the way back. Canned fruits in syrup make fine snacks and provide the three essentials, something solid, something liquid, something sweet. Non-meltable candy bars are also good to have along. Supplies for heavier meals that can be prepared without an excess of pots and pans will help cut down the load. Hot dogs on buns, for instance, are filling, lightweight, compact, and ordinarily will provide several meals. Coffee can always be prepared in an empty fruit can. Be sure, however, to take a can opener. Other items might include matches, snakebite kit, signal mirror, flashlight, and Morse code. Blisters are a common hazard, especially on the steep, downward slopes, and can become painful if not properly cared for. Boots should be sturdy, well-fitting, and adequately broken in. Take plenty of Band-Aids and a change of socks. United States Geological Survey topographic maps are another necessity and should be studied carefully before the trip and along the way when the route is in doubt. Of all these things, the water supply remains the most important.

In case of emergency, three fires, or three of anything, is the signal for distress. Two of anything means all is well. A man can survive two days at 125° on two quarts of water *if no walking is done and he stays in the shade.* So if you have checked properly with the rangers and *remain on your route,* a search party will be sent when you are 24 hours overdue. Aside from dehydration and heat ailments, the most common hazards are fractures, sprains, and loss of way. It is quite easy to slip on a loose rock and be thrown off-balance by your pack. Leg fractures are most likely in rock slides where one foot may become trapped as the other stumbles. Temporary loss of way can be expected along even the best of the old trails. It is best not to proceed far without being positive that you have regained the route. This may mean retracing your steps. Remember that major cliffs or even a 10-foot shelf can only be descended where there is a fracture or slide, and that the trail itself will go out of its way to seek these rare passages. At the bottom of such descents it is always good to build a cairn or to note the terrain well for the return trip. If you lose your way entirely, or if other emergencies occur, get as close to the trail as possible, find shade, construct fires or other signals, listen for aircraft, *stay calm,* and above all, *stay where you are, help will be sent.*

You may wish to enter into a contract with a charter airline to have your progress checked. Prearranged air-ground distress signals might include signal mirror or the conventional Civil Aeronautic Administration emergency signals. The latter are as follows, and should be at least 8 feet long (laid out with clothes, bedding, brush, orange crepe paper, or dug into the sand):

X Unable to proceed
F Require food and water
I Serious injury, need doctor

For the enjoyment of all visitors, you are requested to leave this Park in as good, or in a better condition, than you found it. Park regulations prohibit the destruction, injury, defacement, removal, or disturbance in any way of any public building, sign, or equipment; trees, flowers, or vegetation; *rocks* or *mineral formation;* mammals, birds, or other wildlife; any archeological ruin or relic. Carry your litter until it may be put in strategically placed trash cans along the trails or on the Rim. Other regulations are:

1. Dogs or cats are not permitted within the Canyon.

2. Motorized vehicles or bicycles are prohibited on Park trails.

3. Do not take shortcuts or roll rocks.

4. In case of accident, notify Chief Park Ranger's Office, phone 2477, as soon as possible.

5. When meeting mule strings, stand quietly on the outside of the trail or obey instructions of the mule guide. This is a safety measure to protect both you and the people in the mule parties.

6. All persons hiking *within* the Grand Canyon except on the Bright Angel and Kaibab Trails must have a hiking permit, issued at a Ranger Station, giving their route and expected time of return. They must be suitably equipped and physically able for the proposed trip. All Inner Canyon travel is at the hiker's own risk.

INNER CANYON TRAILS

The physical descriptions of the individual trails, given on the following pages, are not intended as guides but as possible aids. Nor does the amount of space devoted to some trails indicate greater interest for the hiker, only that the trail takes longer to describe.

Bright Angel Trail: This is a 7.8-mile trail that starts near Bright Angel Lodge on the South Rim and ends at the Colorado River. The vertical distance from the South Rim to the River is 4,500 feet. Water is available at Indian Gardens all year, and at the 1½- and 3-mile resthouses during the summer only. There is no drinking water below Indian Gardens. Take a canteen. A campground is located at Indian Gardens 3,200 feet below and 4½ miles by trail from the Rim. Water, modern restrooms, and 20 campsites with tables and firegrates are available.

A hike to Indian Gardens and return (9 miles round trip) is a strenuous trip and satisfies most good hikers. The additional hike from Indian Gardens to the Colorado River and return (7 miles) is exhausting and should not be attempted unless one is accustomed to arduous hiking. (This distance which is approximately 15 miles will take 2 to 4 hours to go down and 5 to 7 hours to come back out.) There are four telephones on this trail for emergency use (River House, Indian Gardens, 3-Mile House, and 1½-Mile House).

River Trail: This trail is 1.8 miles in length, parallels the Colorado River, and connects the Bright Angel Trail with the Kaibab Trail. There is no drinking water on this trail. Colorado River water is *not* safe to drink, and there are few places where the river can be reached since it is ordinarily made inaccessible by its sheer Inner Gorge.

Kaibab Trail: This is a trans-Canyon trail, 20.6 miles from Rim-to-Rim, divided into two sections—the South and the North.

The *South Section* of the trail begins near Yaki Point, 4.5 miles east of the Visitor's Center. It is a steep 7.1-mile trip to the Kaibab Suspension Bridge. Views along this trail are more open than Bright Angel, with vast panoramas of color, form, and distance shifting like an enormous kaleidoscopic vision before the hiker, as the ground falls away beneath his feet. From Yaki Point down, the very trail seems in a hurry to get to the river, using switchbacks and long slopes as alternating devices for losing altitude. There is no water, no green oasis anywhere on the route, but they are hardly missed so enthralling are the vistas and the sensation of treading the rim of an archaic world. At the Tip-Off, the edge of the Inner Gorge, the trail makes its final descent to the river. An emergency telephone is located 4½ miles below the Rim (near the Tip-Off). Hikers often go down the South Section of the Kaibab Trail and return via the River and Bright Angel Trails, but only the sturdiest hikers can make this circle trip to the River and return in one day. There are no campgrounds on the South Section of the trail.

A trip to Cedar Ridge and the Fossil Fern Exhibit, 1½ miles from the head of the Kaibab Trail, makes a good short hike through the Kaibab limestone, Toroweap formation, the Coconino sandstone and through the Hermit shale for a total descent of approximately 1,300 feet. This is a very interesting hike for the amateur geologist since much of the trail is along ledges blasted out of the solid rocks. Naturalist-conducted hikes are scheduled to Cedar Ridge during the summer. For further information, inquire at the Visitor Center.

The distance from the Kaibab Suspension Bridge to the North Rim by the *North Section* of the Kaibab Trail is 13.6 miles. From the Bridge, the trail parallels Bright Angel Creek up the Canyon approximately 9 miles to Roaring Springs. There it ascends the walls of Roaring Springs Canyon for 4½ miles, topping out on the North

Rim where it is ¾ mile (by road) to the North Rim District Ranger Station and 1½ miles to Grand Canyon Lodge. The trail crosses and recrosses Bright Angel Creek seven times between the Colorado River and the Powerhouse. Telephones *for emergency use* only are located on this part of the Kaibab Trail at Phantom Ranch and Cottonwood Park service cabin, 7 miles from the trailhead. Several campgrounds are located on this section of the trail. Bright Angel Campground near Phantom Ranch provides 10 campsites with tables and firegrates. Additional campgrounds are located up Bright Angel Creek as follows: Ribbon Falls, 5.5 miles from Phantom Ranch, 2 campsites with tables and pit toilets; Cottonwood Camp, 7.0 miles from Phantom Ranch, 20 campsites with tables and flush toilets. There are also two small campsites located between Phantom Ranch and Ribbon Falls. Large groups can best be accommodated at Bright Angel or Cottonwood Campgrounds. Hikers desiring to camp along the trails are requested to use only the regularly established campgrounds, leave a clean camp, and be especially careful of campfires. Only a limited amount of wood is available at any campground —carry charcoal or Butane gas stove. Hikers can be accommodated at Phantom Ranch if advance reservations are made (see page 169).

Abandoned Trails of the Inner Canyon—South Rim: While the old trails are all in poor condition, the extent of decay among particular trails varies considerably. It has been said without exaggeration that the Kaibab is a paved highway compared to the Tanner, but that the Tanner is a paved highway compared to the Hance. It is important for hikers to be aware of these differences. A trip down the Hermit, for instance, would not normally be considered adequate preparation for a similar venture down the Boucher. It is impossible to list the trails according to difficulty because it would depend on which types of situations each hiker found more difficult. But a general grouping can be made. Of the South Rim Rim-to-River trails, the Hermit would stand alone in the position of least difficult. Next might come the Tanner and South Bass, and finally the Boucher, Hance, and Old Hance. These last three are in extremely bad shape and should not be attempted by hikers who have not first been down one of the

Clement Powell Butte as viewed from the North Kaibab Trail. Union Pacific Railroad photo.

trails in the intermediary group. Ordinarily, the Old Hance should not be used at all unless in an emergency situation.

As for water along the South Rim trails, there is little—in most cases none. Springs shown on the United States Geodetical Survey topographic map are undependable. In the spring and after summer rains, the Tapeats sandstone (directly below Tonto Plateau) will sometimes capture potholes of water which may be reached by walking down the dry streambeds cutting the plateau, but such finds cannot be counted on. Only the Hermit and Boucher Trails afford permanent water, and then only near the top and bottom of these routes. There is also permanent water in Hance Creek, Cottonwood Creek, and Pipe Creek, and water in Red Canyon during the spring only. No dependable supply occurs east of Hance Creek or west of Boucher Creek.

The *Hermit Trail* is a good introduction to wilderness hiking within Grand Canyon, though a ⅓-mile section of rock slides in the Supai formation should not be underrated. The slide remains one of the more difficult sections to be found along any of the non-maintained trails. The head of the trail is clearly marked and is located at the end of the fire lane that leads west from the Hermit's Rest parking area. The trail is in fair condition with the exception of the slides, which occur just above the descent of the Redwall formation. It is 6.2 miles from the head of the trail to now abandoned Hermit Camp operated as a tourist resort by the Santa Fe Railroad after 1912. A way may then be made to the river by working through a jungle of mesquite for a mile or so along Hermit Creek. Ordinarily a trip to the River should be a two-day journey.

Three other trails also descend into the Hermit Basin, as the topographic map shows. It is an easy, 5-mile hike to the water-and-picnic spot at Dripping Springs. The Waldron Trail is in fair to poor condition, while the Louis Boucher route is in very poor shape. A 5-hour, 1½-mile naturalist-conducted hike down on Hermit Trail (a vertical descent of approximately 1,500 feet) is given daily during the summer. On it or the Cedar Ridge conducted hike (see page 89), hikers planning to make the trips are advised to wear long-sleeved shirts and long pants, comfortable hiking shoes and a hat, preferably a broadbrimmed straw hat. A minimum of one quart of water should be carried by each hiker. No one with known heart or breathing problems should attempt these hikes.

The head of the *Tanner Trail* is marked and lies several hundred feet east of the Lipan Point parking area. This is the longest of the South Rim Rim-to-River routes (12 miles), the driest, and the one offering least shade. The Tanner is almost twice the length of the South Kaibab Trail and contains steeper ascents than anything found on the Kaibab, Bright Angel, or Hermit. The trail is vague but never totally missing for long. The route does not appear on the topographic map and must be traced in from maps at Park Headquarters or Desert View. Parts of the upper two-thirds of the route can be seen from the top of the Desert View watchtower.

The 3-mile *Grandview Trail* to the top of Horseshoe Mesa is fairly popular with hikers, and while rough, it is not otherwise difficult. By any of the three descents off the mesa connections can be made via the Tonto Trail with side trails leading to views of the Inner Gorge. The Colorado River itself *cannot* be reached by means of this network of trails since the spur—shown on the topographic map descending the Inner Gorge west of Cottonwood Creek—is in very poor condition. None of the Horseshoe Mesa Trails is marked, and hikers must find their own way. Vertical and horizontal mine shafts on Horseshoe Mesa contain unexpected drops and should not be entered. There is no water on the mesa.

The *Hance Trail* (Red Canyon) is only 6.6 miles to the River but requires more time and effort than the Tanner's twelve mules. This is without doubt the most perverse of South Rim trails due to repeated efforts necessary to relocate the route. If nothing else, the Hance is a fine exercise in close use of a topographic map. The trail, or what remains of it, is characterized by an inability to see what lies ahead, total disappearance of the way every few hundred feet, and a seemingly illogical route of travel. The trail veers to the right, doubles around corners, and plunges abruptly downward in the most unexpected places. Throughout this erratic course, the route nevertheless touches certain key points that must be attained if the hiker is to continue. Those who cannot stay with the route will only compound their difficulty by proceeding further. There is no water along the way.

The so-called *Old Hance Trail* (the Hance Canyon route), as previously stated, should be used only in emergency situations. Hikers who wish to get into Hance Canyon and to the permanent water available there can do so via the Grandview Trail and east side of Horseshoe Mesa, a far more interesting route. These trails are named after John Hance, an early Canyon pioneer who built many trails in the area. As William "Bucky" O'Neill, another old-time figure, said, "God made the Canyon, John Hance the trails. Without the other, neither would be complete."

The *Tonto Trail* follows the Tonto Plateau from Garnet Canyon on the west to Red Canyon on the east. The trail, however, is not nearly as easy to follow as it may appear on the map or from looking down at it from above. Wild burro trails leading in every direction confuse the main trail. The Tonto Trail between the Red Canyon and Hance Canyon is especially difficult. In going from east to west along this section, it might be of use to know that the crossing of Mineral Canyon occurs where the first major side canyon comes into Mineral Canyon from the southeast. For any travel along the Tonto Trail, allow sufficient time, and carry plenty of water.

The *Bass Trail* is approximately 9 miles from Rim to River. Mystic Springs is dry, and no permanent water occurs along the entire route, though there is sometimes seasonal water at the bottom of Bass Canyon. Dirt roads to the trailhead are passable for pickup or jeep. The trail begins at Bass Camp, about 4 miles north of the Pasture Wash Ranger Station. Like the Hance Trail, it is often very difficult to follow, and care must be taken to be sure the hiker is on the trail.

OLD AND ABANDONED TRAILS OF THE NORTH RIM

The North Rim offers a different type of trail system than that of the South Rim. There are only three Rim-to-River trails (of these, only the North Kaibab, not covered here, is maintained by the National Park Service), and there is no connecting trail along the Tonto Platform to give the system unity. Several of the North Rim routes, notably the Shinumo (North Bass) and Nankoweap, are quite long and in very poor condition. Hikers should be wary of attempting them. It should also be kept in mind that any descent to the River from the North Rim involves a return ascent of an additional 1,000 vertical feet above that which is contained between the river and the South Rim.

The *Clear Creek Trail* ordinarily should not be very difficult to follow. The beginning of the trail is marked and lies one-half mile

94

north of Phantom Ranch. The trail climbs up to the Tonto Plateau, and much of the route follows the southern edge of the plateau. The distance from Phantom Ranch to the campsite at Clear Creek is 8.1 miles. Water is available from Clear Creek.

The *Thunder River Trail* to Thunder Springs and Tapeats Creek lies outside the Park boundaries for the greater portion of the way. Prospective hikers should check with Rangers at the North Rim Ranger Station prior to attempting the trip. The head of the trail is in Indian Hollow, about 18.3 miles southwest of the Forest Service Ranger Station at Big Springs. It is a waterless 13 miles from the head of the trail to Thunder Springs. The trail leaves Little Saddle and drops 1,000 feet through the Kaibab limestone region for one mile, then circles east and then south for approximately 8½ miles to a point where it drops another 1,000 feet into Surprise Valley. It then meanders in an easterly direction for approximately 2½ miles where it drops 1,000 feet in the last mile into Thunder River and Tapeats Creek to the campsite. (Some of the best fishing in the Canyon is available along Thunder River and Tapeats Creek.) The trail is in generally good condition, but there is no drinking water along it. There are good topographic maps of this particular region, and a map showing the principal features is available from the Supervisor, Kaibab National Forest, Williams, Arizona 86046.

The *Shinumo Trail* (North Bass), 12.6 miles from Rim-to-River, is the northern extension of the Bass Trail. The head of the trail is at Swamp Point, approximately 20 miles west of the North Rim Entrance Station, and is accessible only to pickup or jeep. Approximately one mile down the trailhead, the trail forks. The Shinumo Trail leaves the main trail here and heads in a southeasterly direction.

The trailhead of the *Nankoweap Trail* is located in the saddle below Saddle Mountain and may be reached by taking the Saddle Mountain Fire Road. (Permission to use this road must be obtained from the District Ranger.) When the road enters the burn area of the Saddle Mountain Fire, stay to the right (south) along the Park boundary. From the parking loop at the end of the road, follow the Canyon rim quite closely to the trailhead, located in the saddle. While it shows well on the map, the trail is obliterated in many places due to slides and is only vaguely evidenced at the ridges where slides have not covered it. It is a long (about 25 miles), dry trail, and it is very difficult to say the least.

CLIMBING CLIFFS OR BUTTES

Some people have climbed such peaks as the Battleship, Dana Butte, Shiva Temple, Wotan's Throne, and Vishnu Temple. But, before climbing of any cliff or butte in Grand Canyon National Park a permit *must* be obtained from the proper District Ranger's Office. Permission for such climbing will *not* be granted unless all members of the party are properly clothed, equipped, are qualified physically and through experience to make the proposed climb, and unless the necessary water and supplies are carried. Solo climbs are *not* permitted in the Park.

FLOAT TRIPS DOWN THE COLORADO RIVER

The boat-float trip between Lee's Ferry and Lake Mead is another way of seeing the Inner Canyon. This 315-mile journey, which usually takes from 10 days to 2 weeks, is pure, undiluted adventure. But because of the hazardous nature of the Colorado River within Grand Canyon National Park and Monument, a permit issued by the Superintendent is required for all travel upon the waters within the Park and Monument. This permit is awarded only to parties using boats or rafts that are deemed safe by the Superintendent. Also the party must be in the charge of a competent, responsible, and experienced leader who has a good understanding of the Park rules and regulations as they pertain to traversing the river, knowledge of the Canyon geographically, and previous experience on the Colorado River through Grand Canyon National Park.

Several commercial operators offer guided boat-float trips through the Grand Canyon which meet all the rules and regulations of the Park. These trips furnish the guides, boats or rafts, camping gear, jacket-type life preservers (which must be worn at all times on the water), food, etc. For a list of the approved commercial operators, as well as a copy of the regulations and requirements for a permit to traverse the Colorado River through the Park, write to the Superintendent, Grand Canyon National Park, Grand Canyon, Arizona 86023.

Chapter 5.

Plantlife in the Park

VISITORS to National Parks are, in the main, interested in the enjoyment of superlative scenery. But mountains, lakes, glaciers, and sunsets alone do not constitute scenery. Without the forests, the flower-filled fields, and the animals that inhabit them, these remaining vestiges of the once great American wilderness would be barren indeed. People are gradually learning that a richer, deeper enjoyment of these scenic areas may be derived through acquiring a basic knowledge of the magnificent manifestations of Nature represented there. In Grand Canyon National Park, climatic conditions have provided a great variety of habitats which enable the visitor to find concentrated here a wealth of plant and animal life.

LIFE ZONES

Late in the nineteenth century, Dr. C. Hart Merriam, after studying this area, proposed the life-zone concept. The surface of the North Hemisphere can be divided into seven major Life Zones: Subtropical, Lower Sonoran, Upper Sonoran, Transition, Canadian, Hudsonian, and Arctic-Alpine.

From the bottom of Grand Canyon to an altitude of about 4,000 feet, climatic conditions are similar to those encountered at sea level in northern Mexico. At these elevations are found plant-and-animal associations characteristic of the hot, desert climate, therefore the belt is known as the Lower Sonoran Life Zone. From about 4,000 to 7,000 feet in altitude, within the Canyon, conditions prevail which are characteristic of central United States and are referred to as the Upper Sonoran Life Zone. Between 7,000 and 8,000 feet, they resemble those of northern United States and the belt is known as the

Transition Life Zone. From about 8,000 to 9,000 feet, the environment is similar to that of southern Canada, so the term Canadian Life Zone has been applied. On the North Rim, at above 9,000 feet, conditions of environment such as would be found in northern parts of Alaska and Canada prevail in the so-called Hudsonian Life Zone. Thus, in climbing from the River to the North Rim, you will have made a trip that compares with one from northern Mexico to northern Canada, measured not in miles, but by changes in climate, vegetation, and wildlife.

It must be understood that the elevational limits of Life Zones are by no means hard and fast, but overlap and blend into one another. Furthermore, local conditions of exposure, air drainage, the presence of streams, and other factors may produce climatic islands, and fingers of one zone may intrude deeply into elevations that would normally contain another. Hence, in plant and animal distribution and in life-zone determination, altitudinal variations cannot arbitrarily be followed any more than can latitudinal bounds when horizontal distribution is considered. The table on pages 100-101 is a rundown of the common plants and animals found in the various Life Zones of the Park.

In the Grand Canyon region, there are several special conditions that are present that could cause you some confusion, unless properly understood, in regard to the Life-Zone theory. They are:

Zonal Suppression: The fir and spruce forests of North Rim Canadian Zone extend to within a few feet of the edge of the Canyon, where they are met by Upper Sonoran pinyon and juniper growing on the canyon wall. The ponderosa pines of Transition are seldom present between them, for Transition Zone has been suppressed over much of the North Rim. It is present in extensive areas only on the finger-like points, such as Tiyo and Sublime, or the interrupted plateaus, such as Walhalla and Powell, which extend many miles into the Canyon and which drop below the critical level for Canadian Zone while the slope remains gradual.

It is apparent that it is largely the Transition Zone areas of the Kaibab Plateau which have fallen victim to the erosive northward advance of the Grand Canyon. Continuous exposure of the north wall to the desert sun and currents of hot air arising from the canyon

A portion of the Kaibab forest, with wild flowers in the foreground, on the North Rim. Union Pacific Railroad photo.

Zone	Plants	Animals
Hudsonian and Canadian	Engelmann Spruce, Douglas-fir, Alpine Fir, White Fir, Blue Spruce, Bebb Willow, Dwarf Juniper, Aspen, Bebb Willow, Red Birch, Western Choke-cherry, Dwarf Maple, Dog-wood	Rocky Mountain Mule Deer, Turkey, Bobcat, Ringtail Cat, Chipmunk, Cougar, Coyote, Gray Fox, Porcu-pine, Cottontail Rabbit, Jack Rabbit, Raccoon, Striped Skunk, Ground Squirrel, Dusky Grouse
Transition	Ponderosa Pine, Douglas-fir, White Fir, Rocky Moun-tain Juniper, Aspen, Bebb Willow, Western Hophorn-beam, California Scrub Oak, Gambel Oak, Mountain-Ma-hogany, Southwestern Lo-cust, Dwarf Maple, Bigtooth Maple, Rocky Mountain Boxelder, Cascara, Dog-wood, Singleleaf Ash, Sage-brush	Rocky Mountain Mule Deer, Turkey, Abert Squirrel, Kai-bab Squirrel, Black Bear (migrate into South Rim only—from Flagstaff-Wil-liams area), Pronghorn, Bobcat, Ringtail Cat, Chip-munk, Cougar, Coyote, Gray Fox, Porcupine, Cot-tontail Rabbit, Raccoon, Striped Skunk, Ground Squirrel, Dusky Grouse, Striped Swift, Blue-Bellied Swift, Arizona King Snake

* Exotics located principally at Phantom Ranch, or at Havasu Canyon (within Havasupai Indian Reservation). Although it is contrary to the National Parks' policy to introduce any biological species not originally native to the area within a park, plants and animals have sometimes been introduced prior to the setting aside of the reserve, or have become established even in the face of preventive efforts.

bottom favor the development there of an Upper Sonoran flora. The result, insofar as it affects some species of animals, is that Upper Sonoran species mingle with Canadian species along the narrow mar-ginal strip of the canyon's North Rim, and one not fortified by knowl-edge gained elsewhere might be led to most unreliable conclusions concerning their normal habitat.

Zonal Inversion: The ponderosa pine forests of the higher portions of the South Rim also extend to the edge of the canyon. Here, how-ever, they are met by Douglas-fir trees which grow on a ledge 100 to 150 feet below. The situation at the North Rim is inverted, Canadian Zone occurring below Transition, instead of above. Again, it is the opposite of North Rim conditions; namely, perpetual shade allows a heavy accumulation of snowfall, plus possible downdrafts of cooler

Zone	Plants	Animals
Upper Sonoran	Pinyon Pine, Singleleaf Pinyon, Utah Juniper, Cottonwood, Bebb Willow, Western Hophornbeam, Canyon Live Oak, California Scrub Oak, Rocky Mountain Shin Oak, Gambel Oak, Hackberry, Cliffrose, Southwestern Locust, Arizona Redbud, Hoptree, Bigtooth Maple, Singleleaf Ash, * Fig, * Tamarix, Sagebrush, Rabbitbrush, Snakeweed, Four-Wing Saltbrush, Horsebrush, Hollygrape	Rocky Mountain Mule Deer, Desert Bighorn, Turkey, Abert Squirrel, Black Bear, Pronghorn, Badger, Bobcat, Ringtail Cat, Chipmunk, Cougar, Coyote, Gray Fox, Porcupine, Cottontail Rabbit, Jack Rabbit, Raccoon, Striped Skunk, Spotted Skunk, Ground Squirrel, * Wild Burro, Desert Tree Toad, Collared Lizard, Desert Scaly Lizard, Short-Horned Lizard, Western Striped Racer, Arizona Gopher Snake
Lower Sonoran	Cottonwood, Narrowleaf Willow, Dudley Willow, Yewleaf Willow, California Scrub Oak, Catclaw, Mesquite, *Apple, *Apricot, * Peach, * Nectarine, * Pomegranate, * Plum, * Tamarix, Blackbrush, Burrobrush	Rocky Mountain Mule Deer, Desert Bighorn, Turkey, Badger, Beaver, Bobcat, Ringtail Cat, Cougar, Coyote, Gray Fox, Porcupine, Cottontail Rabbit, Jack Rabbit, Raccoon, Spotted Skunk, Ground Squirrel, * Wild Burro, Desert Tree Toad, Banded Gecko, Chuckwalla, Desert Scaly Lizard, Desert Whiptail, Western Striped Racer, Grand Canyon Rattlesnake

air, which brings about this anomalous situation, these factors locally transcending the effect of altitude.

TREES OF GRAND CANYON

For an area of its size, the Park contains a remarkable assortment of tree life. The presence of a forest, of course, is a powerful influence in encouraging the establishment of many forms of plant and animal life. Nearly all fungi of the mushroom type require a moist, shaded, humus-filled soil for growth and reproduction. Some of the most delicate and beautiful flowering plants have similar habitat needs. Squirrels feed upon the seeds of the coniferous trees and, in harvesting the cones, bury many of them for future needs which often fail to materialize. Thus they aid greatly in the spread and perpetuation of the species. Many varieties of birds find seeds and insects for food, either upon the trees themselves or upon the plants that thrive in their shade. They, in turn, attract the predators, and so hundreds of species of plants and animals become directly or indirectly dependent upon the forests.

Although a general "hands-off" policy toward all forms of life native to a National Park has proved to be most effective in maintaining the natural biological population, it occasionally becomes necessary for man to step in to protect some species from injury. A number of tree enemies are constantly at work among the forests of Grand Canyon National Park. Some of them are sufficiently dangerous to require counteractivity on the part of the National Park Service.

Fire offers the most spectacular menace to the forests. Severe electric storms during the summer months set occasional fires, particularly in the yellow pine belt on both rims. Fires, of course, do provide certain benefits to wildlife and the forest itself ecologically speaking. But, unless promptly controlled, these fires might reduce to ashes many acres of beautiful woodland. Lookouts stationed in observation towers at strategic points and a well-equipped fire fighting organization reduce the spread of such fires to a minimum. Due to strict Park regulations and to widespread educational programs regarding campfires, smoking in the forests, and burning of debris, man-set fires in the Park are becoming a rarity.

It is undoubtedly true that in North America more wood has been destroyed by insects, fungi, and fire than has ever been cut and used by man. Of these various wood destroyers, insects are by no means the least important. In Grand Canyon National Park, defoliators wreak spectacular havoc in some localities, but these pests as a rule do not seriously injure their hosts. Bark beetles annually kill a great many trees, particularly ponderosa pines and occasionally become epidemic in effect. A continuous campaign is being carried on in an effort to control their depredations. Other types of insects do more or less damage but not of sufficient proportions to overcome the forces of replacement through natural reproduction.

Diseases and parasites are unobtrusively at work among the forests but as yet none has done sufficient injury to warrant the expenditure of funds to combat it. Most noticeable of these are several species of parasitic mistletoe which produce masses of olive-green foliage upon the twigs and branches of the host tree. The high percentage of infection among the junipers on the South Rim arouses the curiosity of many visitors.

Likewise, visitors to the North Rim frequently inquire as to the origin of large "bird's-nests" in the tops of many spruce trees on the Kaibab Plateau. These masses of dead twigs are "cancerous" growths known as "witches'-brooms" caused, it is believed, by abnormal stimulation of tree tissue by insects or disease. Such growths frequently bring about the death of the infected portion of the tree together with the trunk and limbs above.

Approximately 40 species of trees make up the forest of Grand Canyon National Park. The more common ones are:

PINYON PINE (*Pinus edulis*). It is a member of the white pine group, usually unsymmetrical in form and attaining a height of about 25 feet and a diameter of 15 inches. The trunk is usually short and crooked with gray, irregularly furrowed bark. The crown may be flat or broadly open with short, twisted branches. The leaves (needles), from 1 to 2½ inches in length, occur in groups of two to the fascicle (bundle). The familiar seeds, known as pinyon nuts, pinones, and Indian nuts are an important food for wildlife and the Indians of the area. The cones, taking two seasons to develop, mature in the fall. Abundant nut crops occur about every three years.

The pinyon is the dominant pine of the South Rim where it occurs in hot, dry localities. On the North Rim it is found fringing the Canyon edge and, usually associated with the junipers, sparsely clothes the Canyon slopes throughout the Upper Sonoran Life Zone.

SINGLE LEAF PINYON (*Pinus monophylla*). This tree has the same characteristics as *edulis,* except that leaves occur *singly* to the fascicle, which is unique among all American pines. It is found in the Park in the Bright Angel Canyon and the Nankoweap Basin.

PONDEROSA PINE (*Pinus ponderosa*). This species is the only member of the yellow pine group that occurs in the Park. It is a massive, straight-trunked, long-crowned tree reaching a height of more than 100 feet and a diameter in excess of 3 feet. The open crown of ma-

103

ture trees is supported on a few hugely developed, grotesquely bent branches. Young trees, sometimes called "blackjacks," have gray-brown to black, furrowed bark, while the older specimens are characterized by red-brown to russet-red, plated bark which shades to a gray-brown toward the top of the trunk. (The bark has the smell of vanilla.) Leaves (needles) occur in groups of three (sometimes two) to the fascicle and are 5 to 11 inches in length. Cones are rough, 2½ to 5½ inches long and 2 inches thick.

Found in pure stands or associated with the oaks, locust, aspen, or white pine, ponderosa pine is a common tree throughout the Transition Life Zone. On the South Rim, it occupies the higher elevations and the courses of cool air drainage, while on the North Rim it covers the warmer flats and slopes, extending below the Canyon edge.

When ponderosa pines grow in dense stands the lower limbs are shaded. Without adequate sunlight, photosynthesis, the food-making process in plants, stops and the limb dies. *Natural pruning* occurs as these dead limbs fall to the ground. Dead and downed trees are usually not removed from the forest in National Parks and Monuments. Although dead they still play important roles in providing homes for many birds, mammals, reptiles, and insects. Woodpeckers and insects help chop up the logs. As decay sets in, needed minerals and duff are added to the soil to make it fertile and water-absorbent. The latter is an important check on soil erosion.

ENGELMANN SPRUCE (*Picea engelmannii*). One of two species of spruce found in the Park, Engelmann has a straight, tapering trunk and sharp-pointed, pyramidal crown with lower branches often touching the ground. The tree attains a height of 80 to 100 feet and a diameter of 18 to 36 inches, although the majority of individuals in the Park are smaller. The leaves (needles) which occur singly are stiff, keenly pointed and four-sided in cross section. They are about one inch in length, remain on the tree from 7 to 10 years and, upon falling, leave a sharp basal knob imparting a roughness to the branch.

This species occurs in dense stands on north and west facing slopes of the Kaibab Plateau. It is usually associated with alpine fir and aspen, and with blue spruce at the lower portions of its habitat. Although found at the upper borders of the Canadian Life Zone, it is considered as a typical tree of the Hudsonian Zone.

104

BLUE SPRUCE (*Picea pungens*). Although it does not grow to the size reached by Engelmann spruce, blue spruce is very similar in shape and general appearance. It occasionally attains a height of 70 to 90 feet and a diameter of 24 inches, although specimens of this size are rare in the Park. It is readily distinguished from other conifers by its leaves which are stiff, sharp-pointed and four-sided in cross section. Trees are symmetrically pyramidal in shape. In comparison with the Engelmann spruce the cones are longer, ranging from 2½ to 4½ inches; the bark is more furrowed and scaly.

Blue spruce is usually encountered in dense stands on the shady slopes of the Kaibab Plateau frequently associated with aspen, dwarf juniper, or Engelmann spruce. On north-facing slopes and in draws it may be found as low as the rim or wherever Canadian Life Zone conditions prevail.

DOUGLAS-FIR (*Pseudotsuga menziesii*). Although not a tree of great size in the Park, where it attains a height of 50 to 80 feet and a diameter of 18 to 30 inches (occasionally larger), this species in the Pacific Northwest develops immense proportions. The straight trunk and broad, pyramidal crown and drooping lower branches and numerous long side-branchlets give the tree a soft, feathered appearance. Considerable variation is found in the bark, which in arid sections is inclined to be ashy-brown and but little broken. The leaves are flattened, slightly grooved above, blunt and protruding from all sides of the twig. They give the tree a furry appearance. The foliage remains on the tree about 8 years. This species is most readily identified by the pendent, cinnamon to reddish-brown cones 2½ to 3 inches long with distinctive three-pointed, trident-like bracts protruding from between the cone scales.

This species is rarely found in pure stands of any extent although it ranges through the Canadian into the Transition Life Zone associated with aspen and the spruces. On the Kaibab Plateau it occurs on the shady slopes of side canyons to below the Rim. South of the Colorado River it is found just below the Rim in cool, shaded locations.

ALPINE FIR (*Abies lasiocarpa*). A tall, narrow, conical tree with a spire-like top, alpine fir reaches a height of 60 to 90 feet and a diameter of 14 to 24 inches. It is, as a rule, small in the Park. Blisterlike resin pockets in the bark of young trees give it the name of "balsam fir." The bark of older trees is thin, flinty, whitish-gray and shallow-seamed. The branches are stiff and extend downward, presenting a dense growth, frequently to the ground. Leaves are flat and blunt except on the upper branches where they become pointed. They project from all sides of the twig, but curve sharply upward. The cones, 2½ to 4 inches long, are purple in color and grow upright on the branches near the top of the tree. Upon ripening the cones gradually fall to pieces on the tree, leaving the core as a small upright spike. This species may be distinguished from the spruces with which it is associated by the flat, blunt-tipped leaves and the upright purple cones, and from the white fir by its small, purple, hairy cones and by its higher elevation habitat.

The alpine fir is rare in the Park and is found only at the highest elevations of the Kaibab Plateau usually on northwest-facing slopes where it is associated with Engelmann spruce. It is considered as an indicator of Hudsonian Life Zone conditions.

WHITE FIR (*Abies concolor*). This, the commoner of two species of true firs found in the Park, is a massive tree with ashy bark and silver-green leaves. It frequently reaches a height of 80 to 100 feet and a diameter of 30 to 40 inches or more. The horny bark is furrowed and ridged, while the straight trunk is gradually tapered and the dense crown is heavily foliaged. The leaves are flat, straight, plump on the upper surface and blunt at the tip, except the leaves on the uppermost branches which are sharp-pointed. They are from 1½ to 3 inches in length and stand out distinctly from the horizontal sides of the twig except on the upper branches where they curve upward. The cones are a pale olive-green with an ashen tinge and grow in clusters standing upright on the branches on the upper limbs. The cones are 3 to 5½ inches long. This species, often called a silver fir, may be easily distinguished from the other conifers of the Park by its long, silvery, flattened needles and upright green cones, and from the sub-alpine fir by its longer, horizontally growing needles, green cones, and lower habitat.

The white fir is quite common and is usually associated with aspen and ponderosa pine on the Kaibab Plateau fringing the Canyon rim and on the cooler slopes below the Rim. It is a tree of the Upper Transition and Lower Canadian Life Zones.

DWARF JUNIPER (*Juniperus communis*). In the Park, this species is a sprawling shrub with slender, half-prostrate stems. The lustrous, green, sharp-pointed, needle-like, lance-shaped leaves are chalky white above and spread widely from triangular branchlets in groups of threes. They remain for 5 or 6 years. The berry-like fruits mature the second season when they become a dark blue, coated with a whitish bloom. Among the aspens and conifers of the Kaibab Plateau, dwarf juniper occurs as a low-growing shrub of the Canadian Life Zone.

UTAH JUNIPER (*Juniperus osteosperma*). This is a low, short-trunked, bushy tree 12 to 20 feet in height, occasionally reaching a diameter of 36 inches. The crown is wide, rounded, open and made up of numerous crumpled limbs. The thin, whitish-brown bark is composed of long strips or scales. The tiny, sharp, scale-like leaves of a pale yellowish-green occur mostly in alternately opposite pairs closely overlapping each other in four rows. They remain on the tree for 10 or 12 years. The berry-like fruits which mature the second year have a tough, smooth, red-brown skin covered with a whitish bloom. It is widely used by Hopi and Navajo Indians; red dye is extracted from the roots; shredded bark serves as diapers and padding for Indian cradle-boards. Juniper "berries" are really tiny soft cones. At Grand Canyon it grows at elevations of 4,000 to 8,000 feet. Juniper is often mistakenly called "cedar."

Characteristic of the semi-arid Upper Sonoran Life Zone, the Utah juniper is usually found in association with the pinyon pine and cliff rose. It is very abundant on the Coconino Plateau east of the Grandview section and west of Rowes Well, especially on the Great Thumb.

ROCKY MOUNTAIN JUNIPER (*Juniperus scopulorum*). Although similar in general appearance to the Utah juniper, this species of smaller diameter, usually reaches a height of 15 or 20 feet and a diameter of 12 to 18 inches. The crown is slender with drooping branch ends. Leaves are similar to those of the Utah juniper although smaller and each usually has on its back a long, indistinct pit. The mature, oval fruit which usually contains two seeds is smooth, clear blue due to a whitish bloom over the thin blackish skin.

Rocky Mountain juniper, which often is wrongly called the Rocky

107

Mountain red cedar, occurs on the North Rim at the extremities of points and promontories along the edge of the Canyon in association with pinyon pine, cliff rose, mountain mahogany and other plants of the Transition Life Zone.

ASPEN (*Populus tremuloides*). It is highly improbable that anyone will confuse this slender, graceful, white-barked tree with any other species in the Park, although many visitors feel that it must be a birch. It commonly attains a height of 20 to 40 feet and a diameter of 8 to 12 inches. The thin, fleshy bark is a clear chalky to yellowish white except at the base of large trees where it becomes thick, hard, furrowed and gray-black. The leaves, which are small, are a yellow-green above, paler beneath, and become a golden-yellow in the fall ranging in some trees to bronze, orange, and red. Trembling and quivering in the slightest breeze, they have given to the tree its name of "Quaking Aspen."

The aspen is perhaps the most conspicuous tree of the Kaibab Plateau where it grows in widespread, open stands on the sun-drenched slopes from the Canyon Rim to the highest elevations. It is often associated with ponderosa pine but also intermingles commonly with firs and spruces and occurs in pure stands. It is a tree of the Upper Transition and Canadian Life Zones.

COTTONWOOD (*Populus fremontii*). The characteristically bowed or leaning position together with the forked trunk usually clear of branches for half its height, and the thick, leathery, shiny-green leaves —commonly heart-shaped—with their flat yellow stems serve to distinguish this tree of the side-canyon stream banks. In Grand Canyon National Park the tree rarely exceeds a height of 50 feet and a diameter of 24 inches. The thick limbs and drooping branchlets form a wide, round-topped, open crown. The thick, grayish-brown bark of older trees is tough and deeply furrowed.

Cottonwood is common to watercourses of the Sonoran Life Zones in the Park. It is frequently encountered along Bright Angel Creek from Roaring Springs to the Colorado River. Several specimens in Grand Canyon Village were probably planted by man and thrive as long as they obtain sufficient water. Others at Hermit Camp flourished until the camp was abandoned when they died for lack of water. A small grove furnishes welcome shade at Indian Gardens and the trees are numerous about Phantom Ranch.

108

BEBB WILLOW (*Salix bebbiana*). As found in Grand Canyon National Park, Bebb willow is usually a shrub although within its range it attains a height of from 20 to 50 feet. The leaves are long and slender, quite pointed at the tip with a blunt base. They are shiny green above. The catkins are long, especially the staminate which is from 1½ to 4½ inches in length and is quite yellow in color. Leaves are from 2 to 7 inches in length and vary in width from ⅝ to 1¼ inches.

Bebb willow is located around Point Imperial on the North Rim and is reported as occurring along streams and canyons from the Upper Sonoran through the Canadian Life Zones. It, or similar species, occur in moist locations on the Kaibab Plateau.

NARROWLEAF WILLOW (*Salix exigua*). This species, often called the coyote willow, occurs as a shrub in the Park. It ranges from 6 to 16 feet in height with leaves linear to narrowly lanceolate, bluish-green in color, somewhat hairy particularly beneath, 1 to 3 inches long and ½ to 1/6 of an inch in width. The narrowleaf willow is fairly common in the vicinity of Phantom Ranch.

DUDLEY WILLOW (*Salix gooddingii*). In Grand Canyon this species is a tall shrub but within its range it reaches a height of from 20 to 50 feet. It is characterized by branches brittle at the base, leaves narrowly lanceolate and very long-pointed, 2 to 7 inches long and from 1/6 to ¾ of an inch wide. Leaf bases and leaf stems are not glandular. The bark of larger trees is rough and dark. Pistillate catkins are from ¾ to 1¼ inches long. This willow is fairly abundant along the lower course of Bright Angel, Shinumo and Nankoweap Creeks and along other streams of the Lower Sonoran Life Zone.

YEWLEAF WILLOW (*Salix taxifolia*). It is a tall shrub having leaves about twice as long as broad and about ¼ to 1 inch in length, the leaves finely pubescent. Its leaves are pale yellow. It is not a common willow in the Park, but it can be found in the Lower Sonoran Life Zone in locations like the Hermit Canyon near Santa Maria Spring.

RED BIRCH (*Betula fontinalis*). It is commonly found in the Park as a bushy shrub but occasionally occurs as a slender, graceful tree 10 to 15 feet high and 2 to 3 inches in diameter, usually growing in spreading clusters. It is readily distinguished by its shiny, old-copper-colored bark and the upright, scaly fruiting "cones." The thinly foliaged crown is composed of very slender branches with delicate, pendent twigs. Mature leaves show minute dots on the lighter-green under surfaces. The fruiting "cones," which are ripe in early summer, are ⅞ to 1¼ inches long. The wood is light, yellowish-brown with a thick layer of white sapwood. The bark is tight, smooth, and does not peel naturally.

Usually found near springs in cool canyon bottoms, red birch frequents moist locations on the Kaibab Plateau. It has been observed at Bright Angel Spring and at South Big Spring. It has not been reported from the South Rim, where its presence is unlikely as it is a tree of the Canadian Life Zone.

WESTERN HOP HORNBEAM (*Ostrya knowltoni*). A slender tree 10 or 12 feet in height, hop hornbeam has scaly, light ashy-gray bark and simple rounded leaves with double-serrate edges and fine teeth. Leaves are 1 to 2 inches in length and resemble those of the beech. The fruit is a nutlet within a green-to-brown, papery, bag-like involucre which shatters readily when ripe. A cluster of these fruits resembles a hop. This species occurs beneath both rims along several of the Canyon trails in the Upper Sonoran Life Zone and extending into the lower portions of the Transition Life Zone.

CANYON LIVE OAK (*Quercus palmeri*). One of the evergreen or "live" oaks, this variety ranges in size from a low, dense chaparral to a wide-spreading tree. In canyon bottoms it is usually 15 to 20 feet high, slender, with a small crown. Trunk bark is soft and scaly. The wide leaves are thick, stiff, circular in outline, with prominent, large, spine-pointed teeth. The acorns are usually sharply conical, often long-stemmed with shallow cups. The wood is brown, heavy, stiff, and tough. Leaves remain on the tree for 2 or 3 years and acorns require two seasons to reach maturity. The canyon live oak is commonly found in Bright Angel Canyon.

SCRUB LIVE OAK (*Quercus turbinella*). In the Park it usually occurs as a stiff, wiry shrub growing in dense thickets with fine branches massed and tangled. It occasionally reaches a height of 15 feet with a

110

slender, twisted trunk and drooping, open crown. Leaves, which are evergreen, remain on the tree a full year, falling in the spring. Although variable, they are usually small, stiff and sharply and irregularly toothed with spine-like points. Acorns are variable but inclined to be long and slender. They mature in one season.

This oak is fairly abundant on the Canyon walls north of the Colorado River throughout both Sonoran Life Zones and into the Transition. It attains tree size in Muav, Saddle, and Bright Angel Canyons, but at higher elevations is a shrub. It is also found in Bass and Hermit Canyons, south of the River.

WAVYLEAF OAK (*Quercus undulata*). At higher elevations, this species occurs as a shrub, but lower it is a tree 15 feet in height. Its leaves are broadly oval, 5 to 7 lobed and about 1⅔ inches long with 7 or more pairs of grayish-green ribs. Its acorns are oblong.

Encountered sparingly on the lower slopes of the Canyon, shin oak, often called the "Rocky Mountain shin oak," is found mainly in the western portion of the Park north of the Colorado River. It is apparently an Upper Sonoran Life Zone tree but extends its range both above and below the limits of this Zone.

GAMBEL OAK (*Quercus gambelii*). This species, also known as the Rocky Mountain white oak, displays the major characteristics of the white-oak group having round lobed leaves deeply indented, leaves that fall in autumn and acorns that mature in a single season. In the Park, it ranges in size from shrubby chaparral, forming dense thickets, to trees 20 feet in height and 18 inches in diameter. The deeply lobed leaves are oblong in outline and 1½ to 3 inches in length. Acorns are ⅓ to ¾ of an inch long with hemispheric cups.

This is the common oak of Grand Canyon National Park, being abundant on both Rims where it is usually associated with ponderosa pine and other trees of the Transition Life Zone to within the upper portion of the Upper Sonoran Life Zone.

HACKBERRY (*Celtis reticulata*). Although probably not arboreal in the Park, these species vary from low, densely branched shrubs to short round-crowned trees. The bark is bluish-to-brownish gray with thin ridges and corky warts. Mature leaves are thick, leathery, veiny, and rough. The mature fruits (orange-red to purple-brown in color) are about ½ inch in diameter with a minute point at the top. While fairly rare, hackberry is found on the south slope of the Grand Canyon and in Havasu Canyon.

MOUNTAIN-MAHOGANY (*Cercocarpus ledifolius*). While commonly found in the Park as a broad, low, much-branched shrub, this species occasionally becomes a small tree with a height of 15 or 20 feet and a diameter of 6 or 8 inches. The trunk is short and crooked with large crumpled limbs standing out irregularly and numerous stiff twigs that produce a low, dense crown. The bark is hard, firm, thin, scaly and reddish-brown, gray-tinted. The leaves are evergreen remaining on the tree about two seasons. They are quite thick and the edges curl toward the under side which is densely covered with minute, light-brown hairs. The wood is very dense, fine-grained, exceedingly heavy and hard when dry. Freshly cut wood is distinctly mahogany-red and darkens with exposure. This species, a tree of the Transition Life Zone, is fairly abundant both under and along the Rim on the north side of the Canyon, especially on such dry, sunny points as Cape Final and Cape Royal where it attains tree size.

The littleleaf mountain-mahogany (*Cercocarpus intricatus*) is closely related to curlleaf mahogany, except that its leaves are different. They are small and leathery, with curled-under edges. Their surface coating of hair and varnish are well-equipped to get along with a minimum of water. Each seed bears a long white plume which, when wetted by rain, twists like a corkscrew, possibly helping the seed to work into the moist soil. Indians used the bark for a red-brown dye, and its dried wood for digging-sticks.

CLIFF ROSE (*Cowania mexicana*). This species, often called the "quinine bush," occurs as a large, many-stemmed shrub or a small, scrawny, open-crowned tree. The trunk, usually twisted and sloping, is frequently divided. The leaves, about ¼ to ½ inch in length, are deeply and finely indented, evergreen, glandular, and hairy which makes them feel "sticky." If chewed, they leave a bitter aftertaste, hence the name quinine bush. The blossoms appear at various times from early spring to late fall and resemble small, whitish-yellow, 5-sepaled wild roses. The fruits are hairy and plume-like, usually five in a cluster and, with the leaves, render the tree easy to identify so that it is not readily confused with any other species. Hopi Indians

112

made sandals, mats, and rope from its stringy bark, arrows from the wood, and medicine from its foliage.

The cliff rose is one of the common cover plants on the south side of the Grand Canyon where it is usually found associated with pinyon and Utah juniper. It is especially abundant east of the Grandview district and west of Rowe's Well. North of the Colorado River it occurs in warmer, open locations along the Rim and below, being particularly abundant in the west portion toward Kanab Canyon.

WESTERN CHOKECHERRY (*Prunus virginiana demissa*). This species commonly occurs as a tree-like shrub in dense thickets and occasionally becomes a slender tree reaching a height of 20 or 25 feet and a diameter of 6 or 8 inches. Trunks of young trees are smooth, later becoming seamed and scaly as the bark turns from brown to gray. The leaves are thick, leathery, and dull-green, being smooth and shiny above, paler and minutely hairy beneath. Leaves and twigs when bruised give off a strong odor similar to that of peach pits. The white flowers are borne in dense, cylindrical clusters and it has shiny, blackish fruits. It is found only on the North Rim of the Park.

CATCLAW (*Acacia greggii*). This is a short-trunked, much-branched, broad-crowned tree, usually 10 to 20 feet in height and from 2 to 8 inches in diameter. The angled twigs are minutely hairy and light reddish-brown, lined with 10 to 20 opposite leaflets which are three-nerved and more or less hoary with minute hairs. The pale-brown pods, flat and twisted, ripen in August when they contain shiny, deep-brown, almost circular seeds. The pods remain on the branches for 6 or 8 months. The sharp hooked thorns, from which the tree derives its name, occur at frequent intervals on branches and twigs. Catclaw is one of the few species that grows large enough to be worthy of the name tree which can be found in the Lower Sonoran Life Zone in the Park.

MESQUITE (*Prosopis juliflora*). Mesquite occurs in the Park as a shrub or small, short-trunked tree 15 to 20 feet high and 6 to 10 inches in diameter. The branches and leaf-stems, with 6 to 60 pairs of opposite leaflets ½ to 2 inches long, are smooth. The fragrant, yellow flowers with smooth calyx appear in May, June, and July. The yellowish, straight, plump seed pods, 4 to 6 inches long, contain

113

6 to 20 hard, brown, shiny seeds embedded in a sweet, edible pulp. The sharp, straight, spike-like thorns occur in pairs in the leaf-stem axils. Mesquite is readily confused with catclaw, but may be identified by the straight thorns, larger leaflets, and the plump, straight seed pods.

One of the few Lower Sonoran Life Zone trees, mesquite grows along the banks of the Colorado River and to some extent on flats flanking the tributary streams near their junction with the Colorado.

SOUTHWESTERN NEW MEXICO LOCUST (*Robinia neomexicana*). In the Park, this species varies in size from a vine-like shrub to a slender tree 25 feet in height and 6 to 8 inches in diameter. The fragrant, showy, pale-lavender, wisteria-like blossoms appear in June and the trees occasionally rebloom in August. The leaves are pinnate, with oval leaflets ½ to ¾ of an inch long. The red-brown, hairy pods are 3 to 4 inches in length and grow in small but dense clusters. The bark and twigs are dotted with sharp thorns.

Associated with Rocky Mountain white oak, Southwestern locust forms the dense chaparral thickets of the Kaibab Plateau fringing the Canyon rim. As it is a Transition Zone tree extending normally but slightly into the Upper Sonoran, it is rare on the South Rim.

ARIZONA REDBUD (*Cercis occidentalis arizonica*). Although commonly shrubby in the Park, Arizona redbud occasionally reaches tree size, being 10 to 12 feet tall and 2 or 3 inches in diameter. The single trunk is covered with smooth, gray bark and the mature twigs and branches are smooth throughout. The leaves are thick, heart-shaped and have 3 to 5 prominent veins. The small, sweet-pea-shaped blossoms occur in clusters of clear magenta covering the branches with a brilliant flame in March and April. The fruit is a thin, flat, russet-brown pod with small, hard, brown, bean-like seeds.

Redbud is fairly common throughout the lower portion of the Upper Sonoran Life Zone in the deep tributary canyons on both sides of the Colorado River.

HOPTREE (*Ptelea angustifolia*). Where found in the Park, hoptree occurs as a tall shrub or small tree with smooth, dark-colored bark ranging from greenish-yellow to red-brown on the young shoots. The bark and leaves are strongly scented. Leaves are three-lobed and

114

pointed. The greenish-yellow flowers are small, cymose, and mature to a flattened, 2- to 4-seeded, disc-shaped, papery samara (wing-like scale).

Finding a suitable habitat in the Upper Sonoran Life Zone, hop-tree occupies tributary canyons on both sides of the Colorado River beneath the Rims. It is abundant along the Grandview Trail, Bright Angel Trail, and along Bright Angel Canyon in the vicinity of Roaring Springs.

DWARF MAPLE (*Acer glabrum*). As its name implies, the dwarf maple is commonly a sturdy shrub and it rarely reaches tree size within the Park. The trunk bark is smooth and gray to reddish-brown. Mature buds and twigs are smooth and rich reddish-brown. Mature leaves vary in depth of indentation, are smooth and shiny above and pale-green beneath with yellowish veins. They are 3- to 5-lobed, the lobes being sharply pointed. Leaf stems are frequently clear red. Fruit is rose-red before ripening but turns to russet-brown.

Although relatively rare in the Park, dwarf maple is occasionally encountered in sunny, semi-moist locations of the Transition and Lower Canadian Life Zones along the North Rim.

BIGTOOTH MAPLE (*Acer grandidentatum*). Usually encountered as a medium-sized tree up to 50 feet in height and 12 inches in diameter, bigtooth maple occupies moist and shaded locations. The bark is smooth and gray to grayish-brown. The flowers, which precede the leaves, are broadly oblong with several teeth broadest near the apex. The fruit has an especially long wing, 1 inch or more. It is possible to confuse this species with dwarf maple; however, the broadly-lobed leaves and the larger size of the tree are usually sufficient characteristics for identification.

The bigtooth maple occurs in the Park as a small, spreading tree in shaded locations near springs in the Transition and Upper Sonoran Life Zones. It is not reported from above the Rim and occurs mainly on the north side of the Colorado River although found occasionally south of the River where climatic and moisture conditions favor its growth.

ROCKY MOUNTAIN BOXELDER (*Acer negundo interius*). Usually found as a medium-sized tree, this member of the maple genus

115

reaches a height of from 20 to 50 feet with a diameter of 10 to 30 inches. The trunk is short and clear supporting a broad, dense, rounded, usually drooping crown. The bark is a pale grayish-brown with regular furrows and narrow ridges. The mature season's twigs are thickly coated with downy hairs as are the three-parted leaves, sometimes on both surfaces, always beneath. The greenish flowers differ from the other maples in being single-sexed and only one sex to the tree. Seeds remain on the twigs until well into the winter.

The box elder is similar in its choice of habitat to bigtooth maple, preferring moist although sunny locations in the Transition Life Zone. It is abundant near Cliff Springs on the North Rim and in the upper portions of Bright Angel Canyon and Roaring Springs Canyon.

CASCARA (*Rhamnus betulaefolia*). Found only in the Park as a dense-clumped shrub, cascara in its range becomes a widely branched tree over 30 feet tall with a trunk 20 to 30 inches in diameter. The trunk bark is smooth and brown to ashy-gray, while that of the twigs is a dull red-brown and may be somewhat hairy. The mature leaves are rather leathery with pronounced hairiness on the veins and leaf stems. The veins are conspicuously connected in a network. The fruits are cherry-like and red, ripening to black. Within the thin, juicy, sweetish pulp are 2 to 3 hard, smooth, olive-green seeds which are flattened where they come in contact with each other. The oval leaves, rounded at the tip, are about the same width throughout and persist late into the autumn.

As a shrub, this species is reported from the upper portions of Roaring Springs Canyon where it is found under Transition Zone conditions.

DOGWOOD (*Cornus stolonifera*). This species very rarely reaches tree size and, as far as is known, is never more than a bushy shrub in the Park. The branches and twigs are markedly reddish-brown in hue, the leaves are short-stemmed and oval and the flowers are small and closely grouped in a flat cyme. The berry-like fruits are borne in flat, open clusters. Dogwoods are on the North Rim and near Bright Angel Spring.

SINGLELEAF ASH (*Fraxinus anomala*). This tree is usually quite small, not more than 15 or 20 feet in height although larger indi-

116

viduals are in Havasu Canyon. It is readily distinguished from the other ashes by the fact that the leaves are single, somewhat heart-shaped and 1½ to 2 inches in length. The flowers are inconspicuous occurring in an open cluster or panicle. The fruit is a samara or wing-like scale which readily distinguishes this genus from the red-bud with which single-leaf ash might be confused.

The single-leaf ash occurs, in the main, as a tall shrub through the Upper Sonoran Life Zone, occasionally invading the lower portion of the Transition. It is more common north of the Colorado particularly in Bright Angel Canyon.

NEW MEXICAN ELDER (*Sambucus glauca*). The New Mexican elder commonly occurs in the Park as a tall, many-stemmed shrub. It occasionally reaches a height of 15 or 20 feet with a trunk diameter of 4 to 8 inches. The lower branches are arched and drooping giving the tree a broad, rounded crown. The thin, yellowish-brown bark is deeply cut into a network of narrow, connecting ridges. The season's twigs are smooth, reddish-brown, angled and marked with large, horseshoe-shaped leaf scars. The mature leaves are composed of 3 to 9 leaflets, lighter green beneath. The small, cream-colored blossoms form a conspicuous, open cyme. Mature berries appear whitish from a chalky bloom which, when rubbed off, exposes a blue-black skin. The fruit occurs in drooping open clusters and is edible. The berries are 1- to 3-seeded and have a sweetish flavor.

The New Mexican elder occurs as a large shrub or small tree in the Transition Life Zone. It is abundant on the Walhalla Plateau and just back of the rim on the north side of the Canyon. It has been reported occasionally from the South Rim.

WILDFLOWERS IN THE PARK

The flora of the Lower Sonoran Life Zone is of particular interest, not only to the botanist but also to the casual observer. Profuse and rank growth is not in evidence, and by far the most abundant plant is burrobrush (*Hymenoclea salsola*). This low, much-branched shrub, usually 2- to 4-feet high, has a white or straw-colored bark and green twigs. Its densely-hairy fruit armed with spines is more conspicuous than its silvery-red blossoms.

Among other shrubs of this Zone are blackbrush, rabbit brush, manzanita, and four-wing saltbrush, although the last three are more common in the Zone above. Among the most common flowers to be found on the lower stretches of the Canyon are wild four-o'clock, jimson weed, blue larkspur, locoweed, scarlet mallow, milkweed, wild mustard, nightshade, golden smoke, desertplume, Indian paintbrush, white Pentstemon, prickly phlox, primrose, wild sweet pea, and poppy thistle.

Several species of cacti are typical of this Lower Sonoran Zone; among these are the so-called barrelcactus, the buckhorn cholla, the hedge-hog cactus, the banana cactus, several varieties of the prickly pear, and the agave or century-plant. (The latter does not take 100 years to bloom but dies once it blooms. It sometimes grows as much as 6 inches daily, reaching heights of 12 feet or more.) In no hothouse or cultivated rose garden can you usually expect to view blooms more delicate and beautiful than those on the various cacti. They first appear at the bottom of the Canyon in early April in a great variety of colors and shades—yellow, pink, red, purple, and mauve. A great patch of cactus in full bloom is one of the rarest and most beautiful sights that Mother Nature has to offer. Cacti are typical of the drought-resistant plants found in the warm, dry Southwest. The thick, fleshy stems and waxy "skin" of the cactus prevent drying out. Annual precipitation on the South Rim averages 16 inches and comes as light winter snow, and as short, violent, summer thunderstorms.

The most common shrub in the higher portion of the Lower Sonoran Zone and all of the Upper Sonoran Zone, plus lower region of the Transition Zone, is sagebrush (*Artemisia tridentata*). The extensive root system is drought-resistant and the shrub grows to great age. It was a valuable desert fuel for the pioneers' campfires, and was also used medicinally. Sagebrush is also an important food for the pronghorn. Its grayish color is due to a protective "fur" of silky hairs.

Another shrub common to both zones is the green jointfir or Mormon Tea (*Ephedra viridis*). This green, stick-like plant has *no* leaves. It manufactures its food entirely in its stems and got its name from the Mormon pioneers who brewed a tea-like beverage from it.

The common shrubs of the Upper Sonoran Zone are the Apache plume, snakeweed, hollygrape (Fremont mahonia), snowberry, fringe bush (silk-tassel), manzanita and the fern bush. The latter is so named because of its delicate fern-shaped leaves, which, by the way, have a very pleasant odor. It blooms late for this warm climate—mostly in August. Its handsome white flowers attract great numbers of pollenizing insects. Deer will eat it, but not by preference.

The hollygrape or Fremont mahonia (*Berberis fremontii*) was once classified as a tree in the Park, but it is very difficult to find it in any other form but a shrub. Its leaves are like holly and its fruit like small grapes. This species, sometimes called barberry, blooms in June and is used by Navajo Indians who extract yellow dye from its bark and roots.

Several species of cacti are also common to this zone, such as pincushion cactus, beehive cactus, tree cactus, and one of the prickly pears. Here, too, is found the datil yucca and the *Yucca baccata*. The latter is known as Spanish bayonet, which is a member of the lily family. Indians used yucca leaf fibers for baskets, mats, cloth, rope, and sandals. The mashed roots were used for soap, and the white blossoms and the fruits were eaten. The existence of yucca depends upon the yucca moth, the only insect that can pollinate yucca. Without this moth all yuccas would die, and without the yuccas, all of the yucca moths would perish.

The Upper Sonoran Zone is also rich in the growth of beautiful flowering plants, among which are the brownweed, wild buckwheat, filaree, monkeyflower, blue flax, whip-lash fleabane, rock-spiraea, wild onion, goldenrod, wild geranium, sego lily (the state flower of Utah), thornapple, desert ceanothus, sand verbena, spring beauty, golden sage, Solomons-seal, bedstraw, sulphur flower, Western ironwood and serviceberry (*Amelanchier*). The latter belongs to the rose family, and its small purplish berries produced in the fall are eaten by wildlife and were eaten fresh or dried by the Indians. Although it is a useful plant this did not lead to the common name. It was named so because the fruits resembled those of the European Service Tree (*Sorbus domestica*).

In the Park, flowers common to the Transition Life Zone include the alpine betony, scarlet bugler, canyon lupine, locoweed, branching fleabane, red columbine, and blue Pentstemon. There are several flowering shrubs, but one of the most interesting is the silk-tassel (*Garrya flavescens*), a member of the dogwood family. The long, drooping blossoms give the common name. Western pioneers, having no drugstores, used home remedies. They cooked up a bitter quinine-like remedy from the leaves of this shrub, administered for a fever.

The manzanita (*Arctostaphylos*) which is present in two previously mentioned zones is also present here. After fire burns over an area in the Southwest the buried seeds of this plant quickly germinate. Thus within its range, manzanita is among the first plants to cover the burn area and control erosion. Jug-shaped pink-to-white flowers in spring are replaced in the fall by smooth, red, berry-like fruits. Animals are fond of these fruits and in some parts of the country this has led to another common name—Bearberry. Indians use the berries for food and for making a pleasant sour drink.

In the Canadian and Hudsonian Zones of the North Rim, wild flowers add a touch of color through the season. The spring sun takes a while to warm away the plateau's winter chill. By May the blue petals of the larkspur, the yellow of creeping mahonia, or the pink and white of phlox appear. During the summer the reds of scarlet bugler and red gilia attract hummingbirds. August rains bring out a profusion of yellow, gold, and purple in the goldenrods and asters. For complete information on the Park's flowers, obtain a copy of W. B. McDougall's *Grand Canyon Wild Flowers* (see page 184).

A very interesting plantlife found at most of the Park's Life Zones are *lichens* (pronounced LYE-Kens). These are the scaly, gray-green and orange growths found on many rock outcrops. Each of these lifeless looking crusts is really composed of two kinds of plants: a fungus that gives it form and hardness, and an alga (related to the seaweeds). The fungus provides protection and the alga provides food for both. This living together of two dissimilar organisms is called symbiosis. Lichen growing on bare rock produces acids that help dissolve the rock, thus starting the infinitely slow but important process of making soil. Nature has lots of time and has produced much precious soil this way.

Speaking of soil, most of the Grand Canyon soil is a thin layer of decomposed rock. Only the denser forest areas and the side canyons and valleys have received soil by the process of deposition or accretion. Along the stream bank of the Colorado, there are numerous sandy beaches with scattered boulder beds. Rock-slide conditions are prevalent, particularly along the trails that traverse the vertical rock-wall sections of the Park. Rock and mud slides have occurred from time to time in some of the side canyons, notably the Indian Gardens

120

area. The soil at Grand Canyon, while thin, is quite permeable. The generally steep gradient over much of the Park, however, results in heavy runoff rather than deep penetration. Frost depths vary from a few inches in the Inner Canyon area to approximately 3½ to 4 feet on the North Rim. South Rim Village area frost depth is generally considered 2 or 2½ feet maximum. The water table level is several thousand feet below the surface of both Rims. With solid rock underlying most of the Park area, there are no particular foundation problems.

Chapter 6.

Wildlife in the Park

A LL the National Parks are wildlife sanctuaries as well as being scenic and forest reserves. In your dealings with the animals to be found in Grand Canyon National Park follow the rules laid down by the Park Service. The presence of these creatures is encouraged not for your benefit alone but for the enjoyment of the millions of others who visit this area each year. In the Park feeding of animals is illegal. The sweet and starchy foods that constitute the usual offering of the well-meaning visitor are often actually very harmful to the animal. Above all, never tease or otherwise annoy them. They may have to be destroyed as a public menace after they have come to resent this treatment. Hunting and trapping, of course, are prohibited within all National Parks and Monuments.

The first-time visitor to Grand Canyon National Park may be surprised to see so few animals during the day. The greatest percentage of the Park's fauna is nocturnal, and many of those mammals classed as both diurnal and nocturnal are more active during the night time. Because of this a powerful flashlight will be found most handy when watching them. A quiet vigil around a picnic area or near the Rim can be most rewarding. Another successful method is to drive slowly along one of the Park's roads at dusk or early evening. For best results the speed should not exceed 15 miles per hour. Any animal crossing the road in front of the car can be picked up with the flashlight's beam, and quite often will resume its normal activities under the light when it finds no harm is intended.

Zoologists who have made a careful study of Grand Canyon animals have unearthed considerable evidence indicating that this great gash in the earth has acted as a barrier to the movement of many small animals. This barrier, it is believed, is not a physical one, but rather an environmental hurdle. As an example, a certain species of small

Two residents of the North Rim: Mountain lion (below) and the Kaibab squirrel (above). Union Pacific Railroad photos.

animal gradually extending its range northward reaches the edge of the great abyss. As individuals of this species enter the Canyon they encounter a warmer, drier climate. They find a different life zone —one in which the plants upon which they are accustomed to feed do not grow. Although physically capable of climbing the cliffs or crossing the river, they find their surroundings most unattractive, and return to the Rim where conditions favorable to their life habits exist. Thus the extension of their range in a northerly direction is stopped. Because of this, we often see many differences in animals on the North and South Rims, even though they are only a few miles apart. For instance, the white-tailed black Kaibab squirrel on the North Rim is separated by a hostile chasm from its near relative on the South Rim—the Abert's squirrel, with a gray body, gray tail, and white underparts.

The wildlife of the Park can be divided into two great classifications, depending upon whether they have a backbone (and bony internal skeleton) or whether (like the insects, spiders, snails, worms and many others) they either have the hard supporting parts on the outside, like the insects, or have no hard parts at all, like the worms. In this chapter we will concern ourselves with only vertebrates— those animals with a backbone composed of *vertebrae*—which are as follows:

Pisces—the fishes

Reptilia—the crocodiles, alligators, turtles, tortoises, lizards, and snakes

Amphibia—the frogs, toads, and salamanders

Aves—the birds

Mammalia—the mammals

Of these classes of vertebrates, the first three (fishes, reptiles, and amphibians) are cold-blooded, which means that their body temperature changes more or less with the temperature of the air or water in which they live. The two latter (birds and mammals) are warm-blooded—that is, their body temperature is more or less constant regardless of the temperature of their surroundings.

MAMMALS

By definition, mammals are warm-blooded animals with hair or fur, which nourish their young with milk. They are among our most interesting wildlife to both layman and expert alike. The following

124

short descriptions should aid you to identify species of mammals you may see while visiting Grand Canyon National Park.

DESERT BIGHORN SHEEP (*Ovis canadensis mexicana*)

This sheep has big, curling horns that measure at the base from 12 to 16 inches for a mature ram. (Females have slender, short, and slightly curved horns.) They are brown-gray in color and have a large yellowish-white rump patch. The underparts are light colored. It is interesting to note that wild sheep have hair, not wool, as the name might imply.

These desert bighorns were once common throughout the Grand Canyon and are still found along both sides, mainly on the middle and upper slopes south of the Colorado River. Individuals or small groups are occasionally seen from the trails or from the Rim above. Their tracks and trails follow the most difficult and dangerous slopes where few enemies dare to hunt them and where food is ample.

PRONGHORN (*Antilocapra americana*)

A graceful hoofed animal, the pronghorn has a rather chunky body, large ears, slender legs, and short tail. Its general color is buffy with white underparts, black stripes on face and neck, and a prominent white rump patch. Its horns are less than a foot long and consist of a bony core on which a black horny covering grows. This covering is shed and renewed every year. The pronghorn is the only animal in the world that regularly sheds its horn covers. The true antelope—a name often given to the pronghorn—do not shed their horns, but add to their growth every year.

ROCKY MOUNTAIN MULE DEER (*Odocoileus hemionus*)

This deer is yellowish-brown, sometimes distinctly reddish, in the summer, but the winter color is gray. It has a whitish patch on the rump. The tail is short and slender, with a black tip. There is considerable black on the face and about the muzzle. The ears are very large and, with the mule-like tail, give the animal its common name.

Mule deer are numerous on the North Rim and a few, brought over to the South Rim in addition to some that were native there, have increased until the very limited area on this side is now well stocked. On both sides of the Canyon a few go down the trails to the River and even cross over, but their main summer range is above the Rims on both sides.

HARES AND RABBITS

The Desert Jack Rabbit (*Lepus californicus*) is a large hare with very long ears and legs and is light buffy-gray in color with tips of ears and top of the tail being black. They are found in the Inner Canyon and among the junipers and nut pines along both rims of the Grand Canyon, but are rarely spotted among the ponderosa pines.

The Black Hills Cottontail (*Sylvilagus nuttallii grangeri*) is a medium-sized rabbit with short wide ears, rather short legs and short, puffy tail. In color, it is brownish-gray with clear-gray rump, brownish neck and legs. The throat, belly, bottom of tail, and top of feet are white. These cottontails are found on the North Rim, mainly among the junipers and nut pines, but occasionally are found among the ponderosa pines and Gambel oak. They are brush rabbits, but often live in rock piles or broken ledges where they find safe retreats from a host of enemies.

The Rocky Mountain Cottontail (*Sylvilagus nuttallii pinetus*) is similar to *grangeri,* but is slightly larger and darker with more brown on its feet. They are often seen along the South Rim of the Canyon and even in Grand Canyon Village.

WOLVES, DOGS, AND FOXES

The Gray Wolf (*Canis lupus*) is perhaps gone from the Grand Canyon region today. They were at one time very common on the Kaibab Plateau, but in recent years none has been reported. But, Coyote (*Canis latrans*) is still fairly common in the Painted Desert, Houserock Valley, along the Canyon floor, on both Rims.

Both wolves and coyotes are gray animals, although the coyote occasionally runs to a reddish-brown, especially in summer. Both look like dogs at first glance and a great many dogs look like wolves or coyotes. Both have round eye pupils, like dogs. The wolf is large in size, heavier-bodied, with a shorter, thicker muzzle, while the coyote is smaller, more slender, with a more pointed face and slimmer legs. A large wolf may be 5 feet long, with the tail taking up about 18

126

inches of the total, and it may weigh 100 lbs. A coyote will measure up to 4 feet long, including the 14-inch tail, and weigh up to 25 pounds.

The Arizona Gray Fox (*Urocyon cinereoargenteus*), as the name implies, is gray in color with rich buffy-yellow on its sides, legs, and lower parts; some white is on the throat and belly. The total length is somewhat over 3 feet, of which the tail occupies nearly half. It lives mainly in the Upper Sonoran Zone, but ranges frequently into lower and higher zones. While not overly common, it occupies the whole of the Grand Canyon on both sides of the river and may be seen along the trails.

THE CAT FAMILY

The Mountain Lion or Cougar (*Felis concolor*) is large, up to 8 feet long, of which the tail occupies about 3 feet. An adult weighs more than 100 pounds, and large males may be twice that heavy. It is uniform pale-tan to light-brown in color, with whitish underparts, and a black tip on the tail. These lions were formerly very numerous and are still common over the Kaibab Plateau, along the Rim of the Grand Canyon and down into the Canyon in places where the deer winter. Whether or not they cross the river is not known. They feed mainly upon deer and mountain sheep.

The Plateau Bobcat (*Lynx rufus baileyi*) is larger than a domestic cat. The tail is short and the ears bear short tufts at the tip. Its color is rather yellowish-tan with scattered dark spots and usually several black "tiger" stripes. While not common, it is found throughout the Grand Canyon and on both Rims.

BLACK BEAR (*Euarctos americanus*)

It is hardly necessary to describe the black bear, since everyone can identify it at sight. There are a few old records of black bears being seen on the Kaibab Plateau and a few of more recent date from the South Rim of the Canyon, but it is not a resident animal nearer than San Francisco Mountains and Kendrick Mountains on the south and central Utah on the north. The bear that are spotted on the South Rim at times are believed to have migrated there from the Flagstaff-Williams area.

127

WEASELS, SKUNKS, AND BADGERS

The Arizona Weasel (*Mustela frenata arizonensis*) is a medium-sized weasel with a long slender body and a long tail with a terminal pencil of long hairs. Its color is light-brown with a yellow belly and toes, and with a black tip to the tail. In winter, the animal is pure white all over except for the black tip of the tail. These weasels are very rare and are found in the Park only on the North Rim.

The Spotted Skunk (*Spilogale gracilis*) is a slender, much-striped and spotted little animal with the unmistakable skunk odor. Its color is black with six white stripes on the back and sides; white spots on the forehead, cheeks, and rump, and a white tip to its plumy tail. These beautiful little skunks are common throughout the Grand Canyon on both sides of the river in Upper and Lower Sonoran Zones where they live in caves and cracks in the cliffs and under cactus or any dense cover, subsisting largely on rodents, insects, and cactus fruit.

The Striped Skunk (*Mephitis mephitis*) is *the* skunk to most of us, being the most common and most widespread. It has a suspicious nature and does not hesitate to defend itself with its potent scent, which is squirted from a pair of glands at the base of the tail and which may be rather accurately directed to a distance of 15 or 20 feet. The width of the two white stripes is very variable. Some individuals have very narrow stripes, some are nearly all black, while others have such wide stripes as to appear white-backed. The striped skunk is fairly common in the Park along both Rims, but is not found in the Canyon itself.

The Badger (*Taxidea taxus*) is a very short-legged animal, with a very broad, flattened body. It is over 2 feet long, but the tail occupies only about 5 to 6 inches. It is light grizzled-gray in color, with white trimmings. There is a narrow white stripe down the middle of the dark head, sometimes onto the shoulders, and white marks on the sides of the face. It is fairly common on both Rims of the Grand Canyon, but not in it.

RACCOON (*Procyon lotor*)

The raccoon is a medium-sized, heavy-bodied animal about 30 inches long including the 10-inch tail. It is rather dark grizzled-gray with a conspicuous black "mask" over the eyes and 6 or 7 black rings around the tail. Raccoons are rather common along Havasu Creek and have been reported from Tapeats, Clear and Chuar Creeks, and Thunder River in the Canyon and both above and below the Grand Canyon in suitable places where food and clear water are available and hollows in cliffs afford dens.

RINGTAIL (*Bassariscus astutus*)

The ringtail cat is a beautiful animal about 30 inches long, of which nearly half the length is taken up by its long, bushy, ringed tail. It is pale tan to gray in color and whitish underneath. These animals are cave and cliff dwellers and find ideal homes from top to bottom of the Canyon's walls.

PORCUPINE (*Erethizon dorsatum*)

The porcupine is quite different from any other of our rodents and understandably so, since its relatives all live in South America or the Old World. As everyone knows, the animal is thickly covered with sharp, painfully barbed quills which are half-hidden in long, yellowish hair. It is a fair-sized, dull-witted, tree-living animal which moves about slowly and deliberately, apparently conscious of its spiny protection. But let an unwary animal or human hand approach too closely and the porcupine becomes a coiled spring ready to deliver a tail-slap that will fill the offender with burning quills. Contrary to widespread opinion, it cannot "shoot" its quills, but when the point has pierced the skin of an enemy it is more firmly attached there than it is to the porcupine!

The porcupine lives in the coniferous forests of both Rims where it eats a wide variety of plants. In winter when other foods are not available it feeds preferably on the inner bark of ponderosa pines, but it occasionally samples the bark of broad-leaved trees. Where porcupines are too abundant they may do serious harm to the forest by girdling and thus killing many trees. Several examples of porcupine work can be seen along the Canyon Rim Nature Trail.

GRAND CANYON BEAVER (*Castor canadensis repentinus*)

The beaver is a medium-large animal up to 3½ feet long including the broad, flattened tail. The color is a yellowish cinnamon-brown. There have long been a few beaver in Bright Angel Creek, and they have been reported from Garden Creek, Chuar Creek, Kwagunt Creek and at several places along the Colorado River both above and below the Grand Canyon. There are few suitable places for them and little suitable food but they are of great interest where they occur.

Squirrels, Ground Squirrels, and Chipmunks

The squirrels, ground squirrels, and chipmunks are almost everywhere and, as a result, are the animals most seen by visitors. There are three species of squirrels present in the Park including the previously described famous Kaibab squirrel (see page 123). The Abert or Tuft-eared Squirrel (*Sciurus aberti*) is found readily on the South Rim. It is a large squirrel with a big bushy tail, dense fur, and long ears that have long terminal tufts in winter. In summer the fur is short and ear tufts wanting. Its color is dark-gray with chestnut-brown on back, black ear tufts and a black stripe along each side, with white lower surfaces of belly and tail. The third tree squirrel present is the Spruce Squirrel (*Tamiasciurus hudsonicus*) which is common on the North Rim. The color of this small squirrel is mixed dark olive-gray above, white beneath, with a black line separating the two along the sides of the body in the summer coat but not in winter.

There are four major species of chipmunks that can be seen scurrying around the Park. The Cliff Chipmunk (*Eutamias dorsalis*) is found on both Rims, but a sub-species of this clan, the Gila Chipmunk, is the common one seen around the hotels along the South Rim and halfway down inside of the Canyon. These are a medium-size chipmunk with rather long ears and long bushy tail. Their color is rusty-gray with light and dark side-stripes much obscured by gray. The Wasatch Chipmunk (*Eutamias minimus*), found on the North Rim, is a very small chipmunk with small ears and nine narrow stripes along the back and sides. Another common chipmunk on the North Rim is the Beaver Mountain Chipmunk (*Eutamias umbrinus adsitus*). In size, it is conspicuously larger than the Wasatch, with larger ears, broader stripes on the back and a pure-white belly. The fourth species, the Hopi Chipmunk (*Eutamias quadrivittatus*), is common among the nut pines and junipers around the edges of the Painted Desert. It is a rather large chipmunk with distinct striping, pale-gray and golden colors and rich orange under the surface of the tail.

There are several kinds of ground-living squirrels in the Park. The Antelope Squirrel (*Ammospermophilus leucurus*) is very common over the Painted Desert, Houserock Valley, in Kanab Wash, and down through the Grand Canyon on the south side of the Colorado River in Lower Sonoran Zone. They are typical desert dwellers and feed much on cactus fruit and seeds. They seem to be quite independent of drinking water, other than that supplied by their food. Their color is pale-tan with one white stripe on either side; tail is white beneath and curved over body in flight. The Mantled Ground Squirrel (*Callospermophilus lateralis*) makes its home on the North Rim in fairly good numbers. It is chipmunk-like but larger, reddish-brown with a single light stripe, bordered by blackish, on either side of back, no stripes on side of face, but a light ring around the eye. The Rock Squirrel (*Spermophilus variegatus grammurus*) is a large, bushy-tailed ground squirrel with conspicuous ears and coarse gray fur. Its upperparts are rusty-gray with fine wavy crosslines of black. The lower parts and eyelids are whitish, while the tail is gray. They are usually seen on or near the rocks where they make their homes. They use cracks and crevices and safe retreats up and down the sides of the Grand Canyon and out over the open country. The Speckled Ground Squirrel (*Spermophilus spilosoma*) is a small, short-eared, slender-tailed little animal with a rusty-brown back, thickly speckled with white dots. They are common in the grassy parks among the junipers and nut pines over the San Francisco Mountains Plateau, and a few have been seen near the edges of Grand Canyon National Park in Trash Wash and Pasture Wash. They are so shy and protectively colored as to be rarely seen. They live in little well-concealed burrows under the grass and sagebrush.

The Zuni Prairie Dog (*Cynomys gunnisoni zuniensis*) is a rather small prairie dog with short ears, short tail, short legs and a plump buffy-gray body; the nose and spots over the eyes are dusky, while the tip of the tail is whitish. This species of prairie dog is common in colonies or dog towns over the plateau country of New Mexico and Arizona, south of the Grand Canyon, mainly in Upper Sonoran Zone. It comes into the Park at Pasture Wash, in the vicinity of Trash Tank and at other places along the south boundary. No prairie dogs occur immediately north of the Canyon.

MICE, VOLES, SHREWS, AND GOPHERS

There are several species of pocket gophers in the Park. Their family name, *Geomyidae,* means the family of "earth-mice" and defines these animals rather well. The pocket gophers are heavy-bodied

131

burrowing animals, with the front claws greatly enlarged for digging. Their ears are very small, and their tails short and rather plump. Gophers are usually brown or tan in color, occasionally with one or more white spots which seem to be distributed more or less at random, usually on the head. The "pocket" mentioned in their common name refers to the fur-lined pouch on each cheek, which opens outside of the mouth and which is used for the temporary storage and transportation of food. The five species are found in and around the Grand Canyon and are not easy to distinguish. They are very highly adapted to underground life and are seldom seen on the surface. The usual indication of their presence is a loose pile of freshly excavated earth that seems to have come from nowhere.

Pocket Mice and Kangaroo Rats are related to the pocket gophers and like their close relatives, they have fur-lined cheek pouches on either side. As the name suggests, all of the several species of kangaroo rats have very long hind legs for leaping, and very long tails to keep their balance while doing so. The long bicolored tail, white beneath and bright tan above, has a tuft of longer hairs at the tip. The animals themselves are mostly bright-tan in color, with a black line on either side of the face, white marks at the mouth, over the eye, behind the ear, and over each hind leg, and the animals are completely white underneath. Not all the species of pocket mice have such long hind legs and tails as the kangaroo rats, but they are all a rather dark grizzled-brown with white or light underparts. Both pocket mice and kangaroo rats prefer sandy soil, where they dig a maze of branching burrows through the yielding soil. They are seldom seen above ground in daylight.

The Meadow Mouse, of which two species are known to occur in the Park, is a small heavy-bodied animal, from 5 to 7 inches in total length, of which the tail occupies not much more than a third, often less. The fur is rather long and loose, nearly hiding the small ears and the tiny eyes. The animal is dark brownish-gray in color with grayish feet and underparts. One species is common around Greenland Spring and Lake on the North Rim, while the other is found along the South Rim and a few have been found at Indian Gardens.

Woodrats, of which there are about seven different species in the Park, are about 12 to 15 inches long, of which the tail constitutes nearly half. They are slender-bodied, gray or tan above and pure white beneath. Several species have a hairy tail rather like that of a

132

squirrel, while the others have very little hair on the tail. Woodrats are very common throughout the Park, although different species occur on each Rim.

White-footed Mice are the most abundant mammals in North America and this may be true of the Grand Canyon, too. They might be described as mouse-sized, mouse-colored mice with pure white feet and underparts, and large (or very large) ears. They have long tails which are sharply darker above and white beneath. The very-large-eared species seem to prefer to live among rocks, while the others are found almost everywhere in the Park.

Shrews are among the most primitive mammals that can be observed in the Park. While they resemble mice—small, with grayish fur, long tails, and short legs—they are totally different and are completely unrelated. In contrast to mice, all shrews have long pointed snouts, pinpoint eyes, and almost invisible ears. The Desert Shrew (*Notiosorex crawfordi*) seems to have a wide range over the Lower Sonoran Zone of the Grand Canyon.

BATS

Bats are the only mammals capable of true flight. The fore-limbs, modified as wings, consist of greatly elongated fingers that serve as a framework for a very thin membrane. The hind legs and the tail are also connected by a membrane. Until recently the navigating powers of bats were a mystery, as it is known that they can fly with ease in total darkness. Recent research has shown that while the bat is in flight it emits high-pitched sounds that bounce off surrounding objects. These echoes provide the bat with information regarding the location of objects with which it might collide and also probably the whereabouts of insects on which it feeds.

Over 15 species of bats and myotis have been recorded in Grand Canyon National Park. But, for the casual visitor, it is almost impossible to identify the different species.

BURROS

"Wild" burros once were fairly common on Tonto Plateau area. They must be considered "exotics" in that they are not native to the region. The burros were abandoned by prospectors or in many cases wandered away and got lost. Today, a few are still in the Inner Canyon.

BIRDS

Grand Canyon National Park is rich with bird life. Many birds can be seen along both Rims. All-black ravens are frequently seen soaring on air currents rising from the Canyon. Appearing larger than ravens, but with distinctive bare heads, are the turkey vultures. The small birds which may fly overhead with erratic flight are most often violet-green swallows catching insects on the wing, and swishing by like jet planes, are the blackish, narrow-winged, white-throated swifts. White-breasted nuthatches run headfirst down tree trunks searching for insects in the fissures of the bark. Juncos, sparrows, robins, finches, jays, and chickadees are common, too, but it takes quiet watching to see many of them.

The following checklist of birds of Grand Canyon National Park and Monument, compiled by the Interpretive Staff of the Park, is based almost entirely on reported observations by members of the National Park Service and visiting ornithologists. As a matter of fact,

---

KEY:

Location

S—South Rim
N—North Rim
I—Inner Canyon
M—Grand Canyon National
   Monument
*—Specimen at Visitor's Center

Abundance

a—abundant
c—common
u—uncommon
r—rare
(?)—hypothetical

GREBES

Eared Grebe* S:r.
Western Grebe M:r.
Pied-billed Grebe* S:r.

PELICANS AND CORMORANTS

Double-crested Cormorant I:r.

HERONS AND IBISES

Great Blue Heron I-N-S-M:u.
Common Egret M:r.
Snowy Egret I:u, S:r.
Black-crowned Night Heron I:r.
American Bittern S:(?)
Wood Ibis S:r.
White-faced Ibis S-M:r.

SWANS, GEESE AND DUCKS

Canada Goose I:r.
Snow Goose S-I:r.
Mallard * I-S:u.
Gadwall I-N-M:(?)
Pintail I-M:r.
Green-winged Teal N-I-S:u.
Blue-winged Teal N-S:r.
Cinnamon Teal N-I:r.
Shoveler N-M:r.
Canvasback M:r.
Lesser Scaup* S-M:r.
Bufflehead * I:r.
White-winged Scoter I:r.
Ruddy Duck N:r.
Hooded Merganser* S-I:r.
Common Merganser* I:r.
Red-breasted Merganser* S:r.

records of birds are, for the most part, fairly numerous from residential areas, trails, and other areas frequented by man within this region. In more remote areas such as the Tonto and Esplanade Plateaus and great portions of both the North and South Rims of Grand Canyon, however, fewer observations are available. Practically no winter records have been compiled from the North Rim, or from the western portions of the Park on the South Rim. Observations from the Canyon bottom are mostly restricted to such areas as Phantom Ranch and to a few visits made by observers during the spring and fall months. Actually, the relative abundance symbols are general estimates listed merely to aid you in determining which species may be easily observed. The common species names used in this list are in accordance with Roger Tory Peterson's *Field Guide to Western Birds.* (The list also conforms with American Ornithologists' Union's Checklist of North American Birds.) If you have any doubts or questions as to the possibility of a certain species of bird, discuss the matter with one of the Park Naturalists.

VULTURES, HAWKS AND EAGLES

Turkey Vulture N-I-S-M:c.
Goshawk* S:u, N:r.
Sharp-shinned Hawk* N-I-S:c.
Cooper's Hawk* N-I-S-M:u.
Red-tailed Hawk* N-I-S-M:c.
Swainson's Hawk N-S:u.
Ferruginous Hawk N-I-S-M:r.
Golden Eagle* N-S-M:c.
Bald Eagle N-I-S-M:r.
Marsh Hawk* N-S-M:u.
Osprey S:r.
Prairie Falcon* N-S:u.
Peregrine Falcon* S-N-I:r.
Pigeon Hawk* I-N-S:r.
Sparrow Hawk* M-N-I-S:c.

GROUSE, QUAIL AND TURKEYS

Blue Grouse* N:c.
Gambel Quail M:c.
Turkey* S-N:c, I:r.

RAILS AND COOTS

Virginia Rail * S:r.
American Coot* N-I:r, S:u.

SHORE BIRDS

Killdeer* M-I-S:u.
Common Snipe* N:r, S:u.
Long-billed Curlew S-I-M:r.
Spotted Sandpiper* N-S-I:u.
Solitary Sandpiper* N-S-I:u.
Greater Yellowlegs S:r.
Least Sandpiper* S-M:r.
Dowitcher, sp. S:r.
American Avocet I-M:r.
Black-necked Stilt N:r.
Wilson's Phalarope* N-S:u, M:r.
Northern Phalarope* N-I-S:r.

GULLS AND TERNS

Ring-billed Gull N-I:r.
Sabine's Gull S:r.
Tern, sp. S:(?)

DOVES AND PIGEONS

Band-tailed Pigeon* N-I-S-M:u.
Mourning Dove* N-I-S-M:c.
Ground Dove S:r.

(*Continued*)

(*Continued from page 135*)

CUCKOOS
AND ROADRUNNERS

Yellow-billed Cuckoo I:r.
Roadrunner M-I-S:u.

OWLS

Screech Owl* S:u.
Flammulated Owl * N-I-S:r.
Great Horned Owl * M-N-I-S:c.
Pygmy Owl * S:r.
Burrowing Owl M-I-S:r.
Spotted Owl * S-I:r.
Long-eared Owl * S:r, M:u.
Saw-whet Owl * S:r.

POOR-WILLS
AND NIGHTHAWKS

Poor-will * N-I:u, S:c.
Common Nighthawk* S:c, M-N:u.

SWIFTS
AND HUMMINGBIRDS

White-throated Swift* N-I-S-M:a.
Black-chinned Hummingbird *
  M-I-S:c.
Broad-tailed Hummingbird *
  N-I-S:c.
Rufous Hummingbird * M-N-S:u.
Calliope Hummingbird S-N: (?)

KINGFISHERS

Belted Kingfisher* I:c, N-S:u.

WOODPECKERS

Yellow-shafted Flicker* S:r.
Red-shafted Flicker* N-S:a, I:r.
Pileated Woodpecker N:r.
Acorn Woodpecker* S:u.
Lewis' Woodpecker* S:c, M:u.
Yellow-bellied Sapsucker* I-S:u.
Williamson's Sapsucker* N:a, S:u.
Hairy Woodpecker* N-S:c, I:r.
Downy Woodpecker* N-I-S:u.
Ladder-backed Woodpecker* I:u.
Northern Three-toed Woodpecker*
  N:u.

FLYCATCHERS

Eastern Kingbird I:r.
Western Kingbird * M-S:c, I-N:u.
Cassin's Kingbird * N-I-S:u.

FLYCATCHERS *Continued*)

Ash-throated Flycatcher* I-S-M:c,
  N:u.
Black Phoebe* I:c, M-N:r.
Say's Phoebe* S-M:c, N:r, I:a.
Traill's Flycatcher* I-S:r.
Hammond's Flycatcher* N-S:r.
Dusky Flycatcher* I:r.
Gray Flycatcher* I:r, S:c.
Western Wood Pewee* S:c, N:a.
Olive-sided Flycatcher* I-S:u, N:c.
Vermilion Flycatcher I:r.

LARKS

Horned Lark* I-N-S:u, M:c.

SWALLOWS

Violet-green Swallow* N-I-S:a.
Tree Swallow N-I:r.
Bank Swallow I: (?)
Rough-winged Swallow S:u, I-N:r.
Barn Swallow S:r.
(Cliff Swallow? S.)
Purple Martin* M:r, S:u.

JAYS, MAGPIES
AND RAVENS

Steller's Jay* N-S:a, I:u.
Scrub Jay* I-S:c, N:u.
Black-billed Magpie N:r.
Common Raven* I-N-S-M:a.
Common Crow* S:r.
Pinon Jay* M-N-I-S:c.
Clark's Nutcracker* N:c, S:u.

CHICKADEES AND TITMICE

Black-capped Chickadee N-S: (?)
Mountain Chickadee* N-S:a.
Plain Titmouse* I-N:r, S:c.
Verdin I:?
Common Bushtit* N-S:c, I:r.

NUTHATCHES
AND CREEPERS

White-breasted Nuthatch* N-S;a,
  I-M:u.
Red-breasted Nuthatch* N-S:c.
Pygmy Nuthatch* N-S:a, I:r.
Brown Creeper* S-N:c.

DIPPERS

Dipper* I:c.

WRENS

House Wren* N-S-I:u.
Winter Wren S:r.
Bewick's Wren* I-M-S:r.
Long-billed Marsh Wren* I:r.
Canon Wren* I-M:a.
Rock Wren* M-N-I-S:c.

THRASHERS

Mockingbird M:c, N-I-S:u.
Sage Thrasher* I-S-M:r.

THRUSHES, BLUEBIRDS AND SOLITAIRES

Robin* N-S-M:a, I:u.
Hermit Thrush* N:a, S:u, I:r.
Western Bluebird* S-M:a, N-I:u.
Mountain Bluebird* N-S-M:c, I:r.
Townsend's Solitaire* S-N:c, I:u.

GNATCATCHERS AND KINGLETS

Blue-gray Gnatcatcher* M-S:c, N:u, I:a.
Golden-crowned Kinglet* N:u, I-S-M:r.
Ruby-crowned Kinglet* S-N-I:c.

PIPITS AND WAXWINGS

Water Pipit* S:r.
Bohemian Waxwing S:r.
Cedar Waxwing* S:u, I:r.

SILKY FLYCATCHERS

Phainopepla S:r, I-M:u.

SHRIKES AND STARLINGS

Loggerhead Shrike* N-S:u, M:c.
Starling M:u, I:r.

VIREOS

Bell's Vireo M:r.
Gray Vireo S:u.
Solitary Vireo* I-S:u.
Red-eyed Vireo* I:r.
Warbling Vireo* N:c, S:u.

WARBLERS

Orange-crowned Warbler* N:r, S:u.
Nashville Warbler* N-I:r, S:u.
Virginia's Warbler* N-S:u, I:r.

WARBLERS Continued

Lucy's Warbler I:c.
Yellow Warbler* S-I:c, M:u, N:r.
Audubon's Warbler* N-S:a, I:u, M:c.
Black-throated Gray Warbler* S:c, N:u, I:r.
Townsend's Warbler N-S:r.
Black-throated Green Warbler* M:r.
Hermit Warbler* N-S:r.
Grace's Warbler N-S:u, I:(?)
Northern Waterthrush* S-I:r.
MacGillivray's Warbler N-I-S:u.
Yellowthroat* N-M:r, I:u.
Yellow-breasted Chat* I:c.
Wilson's Warbler* I-S-N:u.
Painted Redstart I:r.

WEAVER FINCHES

House Sparrow S:c, M:u, I:r.

MEADOWLARKS, BLACKBIRDS AND ORIOLES

Eastern Meadowlark†.
Meadowlark, sp. N:r, S:u, M:c.
Yellow-headed Blackbird M-N-S:u.
Red-winged Blackbird* N-S:r, M-I:c.
Scott's Oriole M:c.
Bullock's Oriole* I-M:r, S:u.
Brewer's Blackbird* S-N-I:u, M:c.
Brown-headed Cowbird* N:u, S-M:c.

TANAGERS

Western Tanager* M-I:u, S-N:c.
Hepatic Tanager S:r.

GROSBEAKS, FINCHES AND SPARROWS

Rose-breasted Grosbeak* S:r.
Black-headed Grosbeak* N-S:c, I:u.
Blue Grosbeak* I:r.
Indigo Bunting I:r.
Lazuli Bunting* I:c, S-N-M:u.
Dickcissel* I:r.
Evening Grosbeak* N-S:c.
Purple Finch* S:u.
Cassin's Finch* N:c, I:u, S:a.
House Finch* M:c, S-I-N:u.

(Continued)

† Specimen; near Park boundary, South Rim.

(*Continued from page 137*)

GROSBEAKS, FINCHES
AND SPARROWS (*Cont.*)

Pine Grosbeak* S-N-M:u.
Black Rosy Finch* S:r.
Pine Siskin* N-S:c, I:r.
American Goldfinch I:r.
Lesser Goldfinch* S-N-M:u, I:r.
Red Crossbill* S:c, N:u.
Green-tailed Towhee* N-I-S:c.
Rufous-sided Towhee* N-S-I:c.
Brown Towhee N-S:r.
Lark Bunting S:r.
Savannah Sparrow* S-I:r.
Grasshopper Sparrow* S:(?)
Vesper Sparrow* S-I-N-M:u.

Lark Sparrow* S-I-N-M:c.
Rufous-crowned Sparrow* I:u.
Black-throated Sparrow* I-M:a, S:u,
    N:r.
Sage Sparrow* I-S:r.
Slated-colored Junco* S:u, I:r.
Oregon Junco* S-I-M:c, N:u.
Gray-headed Junco* S-N:a, I:c.
Tree Sparrow I:r.
Chipping Sparrow* N-S:a, I:r.
Brewer's Sparrow* S-N:u, I-M:r.
White-crowned Sparrow* S-I-M:c,
    N:r.
Fox Sparrow I-S:r.
Lincoln's Sparrow* S-I-N:u.
Song Sparrow* S-I-N:c.

AMPHIBIANS

Technically, the term amphibian refers to all the backboned animals which spend a portion of their life-cycle in water and the remainder breathing air. They literally lead a double life. In this group are included the newts, salamanders, toads, and frogs. Salamanders and newts are popularly called water dogs, or mud puppies. Sometimes, also, they are incorrectly referred to as lizards. The young of amphibians are found in quiet pools of water where the eggs have previously been deposited in gelatinous stringy masses by the females. Pollywogs and tadpoles are the popular names for the young. Adults customarily inhabit cool, moist, and shaded or dark locations. They are four-legged and have moist skin, which in some forms is lubricated by a thin layer of mucous or "slime." In general, amphibians feed on insects.

On account of their moisture requirements, the distribution of amphibians is limited to the vicinity of permanent or semi-permanent water sources. In Grand Canyon National Park such locations are few. Aside from the Colorado River, which occupies the Canyon bottom, roughly bisecting the Park from southeast to northwest, there are only five permanent streams worthy of the name. On the North Rim, around some of the "sink" ponds such as Greenland Lake, amphibians are fairly common. Here is a checklist of the amphibians of the Park. (The common names of all amphibians and reptiles in this book are those published by the Committee on Herpetological Common Names of the American Society of Ichthyologists and Herpetologists.)

KEY:

Location	*Abundance*
S—South Rim	c—common
N—North Rim	u—uncommon
I—Inner Canyon	r—rare
	(?)—hypothetical

Name	*Abundance*	*Name*	*Abundance*
Tiger Salamander	I-N:u.	Woodhouse's (Rocky Mountain) Toad	I:r.
Western Spadefoot Toad	I-u, N:c.		
Red-spotted Toad	I:c.	Desert Tree Toad	I:c, S:r.

REPTILES

The great group of reptiles, as previously stated, includes the lizards, snakes, turtles, tortoises, alligators, and crocodiles. Of these, only lizards and snakes have been recorded in Grand Canyon National Park. As with the majority of animals, the presence of food, water, enemies, and favorable climatic conditions governs the distribution and numbers. Temperature is of particular importance as reptiles, in general, require relatively high temperatures and a yearly high mean for optimum activity. Their sensitivity to temperature is due to the fact that they are "cold blooded," or that the body temperature is governed by that of the surrounding medium. In cold weather, reptiles go into a state of dormancy or hibernation during which body activities are at a very low ebb. This condition cannot be maintained indefinitely; therefore reptiles are scarce or absent in regions where winters are long. This explains the lack of reptile life at the highest elevations of the North Rim area. Neither are reptiles able to endure extremely high temperatures, and in regions of great heat they seek burrows or shade during the hotter portions of the day. Exposure to the direct rays of the sun for any great length of time may result in death. In regions of excessive heat, some reptiles enter a summer dormancy or estivation. As previously explained in the section on life zones, there is considerable variation among species as to optimum temperature requirements. Some species congregate in "dens" during the hibernation period. Whether this is a social manifestation or a selection of the most desirable location by many individuals is unknown.

Reptiles have developed various protective devices to aid them in their fight against enemies. Several species of both snakes and lizards

139

are able to travel rapidly, and thus escape by flight. Several species of lizards alter the colors of their skins, thereby blending with their surroundings. Some reptiles fight viciously if attacked, hissing and striking at the foe. Some lizards strike a heavy blow with the muscular tail. The chuckwalla has a peculiar ability to inflate its body, which it does after crawling into a crevice in the rocks, thereby making its removal very difficult. Several groups of lizards utilize a very peculiar method of escape. They leave a portion of the tail writhing and twisting, in the possession of the captor and scuttle away to safety. Loss of the tail appears to inconvenience the reptile not at all, and on the North Rim of the Grand Canyon at Bright Angel Point where many visitors congregate each summer, numerous bob-tailed lizards are in evidence. As time passes, the lizard gradually grows a new appendage which is usually shorter and has a smoother scalation than the original. A few groups of reptiles carry an effective weapon in the form of fangs and poison-secreting glands. This equipment is primarily for the purpose of securing food and is used for defense only in emergencies. Of the lizards, the gila (pronounced "hee'la") monster and a Mexican relative, constitute the only poisonous genus known. To date, this reptile has not been recorded in Grand Canyon National Park, although it is found in the Virgin River Valley to the northwest. Several groups of American snakes possess poisonous properties, but the rattlesnake is the only genus of venomous snake in Grand Canyon National Park.

In the matter of food habits, the lizards are, in the main, insectivorous. Of those in the Park, only the chuckwalla is a vegetarian. There are several types of lizards that eat other lizards if hungry. The snakes as a group live upon animals, particularly rodents and for this reason they are of great benefit to mankind, especially in agricultural sections.

Although not a true differentiating characteristic, absence of legs serves to distinguish the snakes from the lizards of Grand Canyon National Park. Lizards are much more abundant than snakes in the Park. During the summer months, they are seen at almost every turn of the trail, whereas snakes are *rarely* encountered. Possibly the rarest are the rattlesnakes, which offer practically no danger to man because of their scarcity. One of the oddities of the snake world is the "pink" rattlesnake, the only reptile so far recorded exclusively from the Grand Canyon. The Grand Canyon Rattlesnake, as it is properly

140

called, is identified by the fact that the colors of the adult vary from vermilion to salmon, which causes it to blend well with the rocks and soil which compose many levels of the Canyon walls. Its range is limited to the area beneath the Rims where it is distributed at all elevations, but it is primarily a native of the Lower Sonoran Life Zone. At no point within the Canyon is it abundant, and considerable difficulty has been encountered in obtaining sufficient specimens to make a careful study.

Reptiles and amphibians should remain unharmed if encountered in the Park. Just because an animal crawls instead of walks is no justification for maliciousness. Everyone is, of course, interested in the proper treatment for rattlesnake bite. It should be emphasized, however, that "an ounce of prevention is worth a pound of cure." Hikers will seldom encounter rattlesnakes on the well-traveled trails, but when they leave the trails for exploring on their own they should take certain precautions such as wearing proper shoes, boots or leggings. They should also avoid stepping or placing their hands near cracks or joints in the rocks which might serve as retreats for the rattlesnakes.

Hikers or campers who make a practice of leaving the well-traveled routes should provide themselves with the latest type snake-bite first-aid kits and should have some training or experience in the proper use of these safety-first aids. Practically all of these kits contain very definite instructions and should be carefully studied by those who travel away from the regular trails in rattlesnake-infested country.

Checklist of Lizards (Key: see page 134)

Name	Abundance	Name	Abundance
Banded Gecko	I:u.	Fence Lizard	S-N-I:c.
Collared Lizard	I:c, N:r.	Blue Bellied Swift	S-N-I:c.
Chuckwalla	I:u.	Desert Spiny Lizard	I:c.
Sagebrush Lizard (Swift)	I-N:c, S:u.	Short-horned Lizard	S-N:c.
Arizona Tree Uta	I:c.	Plateau Whiptail	S:r, I:c.
Rocky Mountain Tree Uta	I:c, N:r.	Lizard	
Side-blotched Lizard (Desert Brown-shoul-	I:c	Western Whiptail Lizard	I:c.
dered Lizard)		Many-lined Skink	S:u.

The Scorpions are often called a "stinging lizard." This is incorrect, because scorpions are arachnida. True, there are over ten species of scorpions in the Canyon, of which one is considered "deadly

141

poisonous." This one is about 2 inches in length, is straw-colored. Its entire body, especially the joints of the legs, pincers, and "tail," are long and slender. It has a streamlined appearance. This is in contrast to the chunky or stubby appearance of most of the non-poisonous species. Fortunately scorpions are not common, even in the Inner Canyon, and are very seldom, if ever, observed by visitors.

Checklist of Snakes

Western Striped Racer	I:c, N-S:r.	Spotted Night Snake	I:r.
Western Patch-nosed Snake	I:r.	Western Garter Snake	N:c, S:u.
		Northern Black-tailed	S:r.
Desert Gopher Snake	(?)	Rattlesnake	
Arizona Gopher Snake	I-S:c.	Arizona Prairie Rattlesnake	I:u, S:r.
Arizona King Snake	I-N:r.	Grand Canyon Rattlesnake	I:u.
Common King Snake	I:c.		
Western Ground Snake	I:u.		

FISH

As previously stated there are only six principal rivers and streams in Grand Canyon National Park: Colorado River, Bright Angel Creek, Thunder River, Tapeats Creek, Havasu Creek, and Clear Creek. Of these, no fish are found in Clear Creek (habitat destroyed by floods in 1950's) or Havasu Creek (calcium carbonate content in the water precludes fish life except for small native *minnow*).

Bright Angel Creek, Thunder River, and Tapeats Creek are considered best for fishing. These are restocked periodically by the State of Arizona, but the results of these programs have not proved overly successful. Bright Angel Creek is the most accessible, while Thunder River and Tapeats Creek are usually the most productive of the sport fish. *Rainbow trout* have been introduced into Bright Angel Creek, Thunder River and Tapeats Creek; *brown trout* have been planted in the same three streams, while stocked *brook trout* are found in Thunder River and Tapeats Creek. No sport fish, except for an occasional rainbow trout and a few *largemouth bass* that migrate up from Lake Mead or down from Lee's Ferry, are found in the Colorado River. The major species located there include the *channel catfish, boneytail, humpback sucker, Colorado squawfish* (rare), and the *mountain sucker*. The latter species is also found in Bright Angel Creek.

Fishing is permitted in Grand Canyon National Park, but an Arizona license is required. Details of regulations, in accordance with Arizona laws, are available at Park entrance and ranger stations.

Chapter 7.

Indians of the Grand Canyon

ALTHOUGH over 800 ruins have been located within the Grand Canyon National Park, we know only the outline of this area's pre-history. Most ruins are of small surface pueblos along the North and South Rims of the Canyon. No large communal centers have been found. Small cliff dwellings and numerous granaries occupy caves and niches in the Canyon walls. A few early pit houses, some ruins of late Havasupai houses, and occasional earth-covered hogans, or Navajo lodges complete the roster.

There is little evidence, as yet, of early hunters or gatherers in the Grand Canyon area. However, in 1957, split-twig figures perhaps representing deer, bighorn sheep, pronghorns, and the like, were found in caves difficult to reach in the walls of the North Rim of the Grand Canyon near Bright Angel Point. These may have been hunting shrines, as no sign of living in the caves was present. Radioactive carbon methods of analysis date these as 3,000 years old. Scattered remains of Basket Maker Indians, also mostly from caves, date back somewhat less than 2,000 years. By about 1,400 years ago (600 A.D.), the potter Basket Makers had settled along the North Rim and a few on the South Rim, which apparently was occupied largely by another group of Indians. These people, whom the archeologist calls Cohonina, were similar in many ways to the late Basket Makers and early Pueblos. Their pottery was made differently, however, and their houses and general way of life were simpler.

By 800 A.D., or nearly 1,200 years ago, Pueblo people from the Kayenta center were building small houses along the North Rim; but on the South Rim, as far east as the present Tusayan Ruin and Museum, the Cohonina still lived. At this time the canyon evidently was a barrier between the people on the North and South Rims. A frontier also existed between Cohoninas and Pueblos along the eastern edge of the Canyon.

The ruin of a Cohonina house, occupied probably about 800, has been excavated near Tusayan Ruin and Museum which is about four miles west of Desert View. The main room was a circular, saucer-shaped depression about 15 feet in diameter. In the center was a fire pit and near it an ash pit. A rectangular framework had been built inside the house. Walls were formed by poles leaned against this frame and perhaps plastered. Three storage pits and two small storage rooms were built along the southern side of the main house. All of these units were probably covered by a single roof. A few feet away was a small separate house which had a wooden tripod framework perhaps covered by matting or brush.

We do not know when this house was abandoned, but by 900 the Pueblos had moved west along the South Rim as far as the present Hermit's Rest. Beyond this, and to the south, the Cohonina continued to hold their ground. During late Developmental times there seems to have been a mass movement into both North and South Rim areas. Many people dwelt in small pueblos and carried on agriculture in terraces built wherever runoff water would supply silt and moisture. North Rim sites show increasing influence from the Pueblo people of Utah. Perhaps nomads were pressing southward, forcing the Pueblos to move on before them.

The Great Classic Pueblo Period probably began late (around 1100 A.D.) in the Grand Canyon area. It had hardly begun before the North Rim was abandoned. By 1175 the Pueblos had crossed to the South Rim, leaving behind their houses, agricultural terraces, ditches, and diversion dams.

On the South Rim the people continued to live, building pueblos containing up to 30 rooms, although most were smaller. One of these, a fine excavated ruin, may be viewed today at a point about four miles west of Desert View. This is Tusayan Ruin, named after the old Spanish Province in which it is located. Here, each summer, the National Park Service operates a small museum and presents daily talks about the archeology and the development of prehistoric man which led to his settling briefly at this site.

Tusayan Pueblo was built between 1185 and 1200. In plan, it

Beautiful Havasu Falls which is found on the Havasupai Reservation in the Park. Santa Fe Railway photo.

formed a broad U-shape, opening to the southeast. Walls were made of unshaped limestone boulders set in clay mortar. A two-story living section formed the western side, four rooms on the lower floor, three above. At the southwestern corner was a partly subterranean circular room, the kiva. (The kiva is used by the men of the tribe primarily for religious ceremonies.) North and south wings consisted of small storage rooms one story high, entered by ladder through hatchways in the roof. In the center, protected by the building, was an open court or plaza. A second kiva was built beyond the north wing of storage rooms, apparently after the first one burned. A bench of clay extended partly around this room. A ventilator shaft through the east wall brought in fresh air as heated air and smoke from the central, rock-lined fire pit rose through the roof hatch. In a line with the ventilator and fire pit was a small hole, the sipapu, symbolic of the entrance to the underworld, cut in the limestone floor.

Probably twenty-five or thirty people occupied this pueblo. Judging from the size of the rubbish heap and the fact that no burials were found, they lived there about twenty-five years. We do not know when they left, but apparently by 1250 this and all other pueblos of the area were abandoned. These people probably moved first into the Kayenta country some 75 miles to the northeast, and then joined the exodus south when drought struck in 1276.

From this point on, our records are few and fragmentary. Sporadic finds of Hopi pottery show that occasional visits into the Grand Canyon country were made at least until 1700, perhaps later. The Navajo, too, visited or lived in the area, for remains of their hogans have been found which date in the middle 1800's. Early explorers found the Havasupai living along the western boundary of what was to become Grand Canyon National Park, the region previously occupied by the Cohonina. Some archeologists believe that the Havasupai are descendants of these earlier people.

Today the Indians in the Grand Canyon region belong to one of five tribes—Navajo, Hopi, Paiute, Hualapai and Havasupai. (Fourteen different tribes are found in the State of Arizona.) The Havasupai live in the western part of Grand Canyon on the *only* Indian reservation to be found within the boundaries of a National Park. (In the Act creating the Park, the lands of Havasu Canyon are specifically reserved for the use and occupancy of the Havasupai Indians.) The Navajo and Hopi live on reservations to the east of the Park, while the Hualapai reservation is to the west. The Paiute can be found to the north and northwest of the North Rim.

146

THE HAVASUPAI

The Havasupai are a peaceful nation whose people say they have never killed a white man. In the twelfth century, their ancestors were driven from their home on the plateaus near the Grand Canyon by raiding Indians, but they found a haven in Havasu Canyon (formerly called Cataract Canyon). Their oasis, 2½ miles long and nearly half a mile wide, is watered by spring-fed Havasu Creek. From its color comes the name Havasupai, or "people of the blue-green water." Actually, the blue waters of Havasu Creek cascade over Navajo Falls, Havasu Falls, and Mooney Falls, presenting spectacles which attract numerous visitors. The large amount of travertine carried in solution by waters of the creek is deposited in small dams of elaborate design below the falls and coats rocks and sticks that project into the stream. The water appears blue in color because of the light refraction from the fine clay particles.

When first discovered by Father Garces in 1776, the Havasupai probably numbered about 250, and at the present time they are believed to total approximately 200 persons. They are closely related to the Hualapai Indians ethnically, and derive their livelihood partly from crops raised on approximately 300 acres of irrigated land which lies along the Canyon floor, and partially from the Tribal Tourist Enterprises. Principal crops are corn, beans, squash, melons, and fruit such as apricots and peaches. Some cattle are raised but grazing land is scarce, in fact hardly adequate to support the large number of horses maintained by the tribe. Most of the men are expert horsemen and greatly enjoy the rodeos and horse races which are a regular part of their program of social events. But, most of their native crafts are gone except for the conical burden baskets that the women still make. Unlike the other Indians of the region who hold tribal ceremonies frequently during the year, the Havasupai have only one major celebration—the Peach Harvest Festival in August.

The Havasupais have the tribal-council method of administration, a method recently adopted by many other tribes. Seven members are elected yearly and the chairman of the council is the most influential administrative officer. The council selects and employs a store manager, a tourist manager, and other representatives as needed to carry on the daily business of the tribe. Other tribal members may and do attend the council meetings and make their views known. But most business requiring tribal approval is taken care of at an annual meeting of the tribe. All men and women who are of age may vote at this

147

meeting. Women take an active part, and one of them has long been a member of the council.

A visit to the Havasupai Indian Reservation and its village of Supai is a separate excursion from the generally visited South Rim area. Access is limited to hikers or horseback trips over 8 miles of rough trail from Hualapai Hilltop, which is the end of the dirt road, 62 miles north of U.S. Highway 66. The dirt road leaves U.S. 66 approximately 5 miles east of Peach Springs, Arizona, or approximately 143 miles from Grand Canyon Village via U.S. Routes 180 and 66. (Caution: There are no services such as gas, oil, auto repair, water, food, or eating facilities after leaving Highway 66 except the services at Supai Village.) At Hualapai Hilltop, you leave your car. There is ample parking space where vehicles and property are safe. A phone at Hualapai Hilltop connects with Supai Village.

Transportation from Peach Springs to Hualapai Hilltop can sometimes be arranged with the mailman through the Tribal Enterprises Office. Mail is brought in twice a week (Tuesdays and Fridays), from Peach Springs. A post office is maintained in Supai; mail can be sent out on Tuesdays and Fridays; the post office remains open during weekdays.

Arrangements can be made for horse transportation from Hualapai Hilltop to the village of Supai and return. Further information or reservations may be obtained by writing: Havasupai Tourist Information, Havasupai Tourist Enterprise, Supai, Arizona 86435. Long distance telephone is possible through Prescott, Arizona; ask for Supai #1, and the Tourist Manager, or if not available, the agent. Telephone service is not always open or clear. It is best to make arrangement in advance. Written requests receive prompt attention, generally, and are less open to misunderstanding. One-half (½) rate for horses is usually required in advance and deposit will be refunded if reservations are canceled in time to prevent horses from making the trip to Hilltop. It will be appreciated if payment for use of horses and other services can be made in cash, although personal checks are accepted. Load limit for packhorses is 150 pounds. People coming in on their own horses must have the approval of the Havasupai Tribal Council. Vehicles such as motor scooters or motorcycles are *prohibited* on trails to Supai.

Accommodations. These are available in Supai and consist of two stone buildings. The Old Tourist Lodge has eleven single beds among

148

three rooms and one enclosed porch, two bathrooms, and one kitchen. The kitchen and bathroom are shared by the occupants. The kitchen is complete with dishes, cooking utensils, running water, large Butane stove, and refrigerator.

The New Tourist Lodge contains three motel-like units, each with a double bed and bathroom. The single kitchen is shared. Bedding, stove, water, and cooking and eating equipment are supplied and are similar to the other Lodge. Electric lights are operated in both a few hours in the evening. No meals are served to guests; they must prepare their own meals. Reservations are made through the Tourist Manager.

Tribal Store. A supply of staple groceries, white gas, and charcoal is generally available at the Tribal store, which is open a few hours in the morning and afternoon. The Havasupai Trading Company is expanding its volume and variety of food items with fresh meats, fruits, and vegetables. These are packed in once a week, and can be obtained twice each week upon sufficient demand.

Campground. The National Park Service provides a free campground with 12 sites. The trail to the camping area crosses the entire length of the Havasupai Indian Reservation. The campground provides wilderness-type facilities and includes picnic tables, charcoal grates, and pit toilets. *No firewood is available.* Cutting of trees or shrubs is prohibited. Campers should provide charcoal, gasoline stoves, or some form of canned heat for cooking. White gas and charcoal are generally available at the Tribal store in Supai Village. Call ahead for information on supplies. Water is available. Camping is restricted to the campground which is reached by trail, 2½ miles below, or down the Canyon from Supai Village.

Hiking. Hikers are requested by the Tribal Council to obtain permission in advance before entering the Reservation, either by mail or by telephoning during business hours, or directly from telephone at Hualapai Hilltop (during business hours only). A trail use-fee is charged each individual, and all visitors must stop at the Tourist Manager's Office in Supai Village to register.

Photography. The Tribal Council has set the following rules regarding the use of cameras on the Reservation: Commercial pictures,

149

either still or movie, must be approved in advance by the Havasupai Tribal Council. They request you write in advance for a commercial permit. Cameras for personal pleasure require a permit which is available from the Tourist Manager. But this does not cover the privilege of photographing individual Indians or their activities. Such photography may be taken only with their consent.

The necessary permission may be obtained by various approaches. If you have the faculty of making friends, try to get permission for photographing on a friend-to-friend basis. Or you may offer to send copies of the photographs. (This is not so effective as formerly, since too many people have neglected to fulfill their commitments.) Or you can bring something to trade with the Indians. (Monetarily, it need not be costly. If it is amusing, from the point of view of Indians, so much the better for you.) While there are other approaches, a modest payment is usually best for all concerned.

THE HOPI

The Hopi Indians are the pueblo dwellers of Arizona. They have a reservation about 631,000 acres in size, which is entirely surrounded by the Navajo Reservation. For the most part their villages are perched on three high, barren mesas located northwestward from Keams Canyon and east of the Grand Canyon. Within this area a few more than 4,000 Hopi reside.

The name Hopi (pronounced Hoe-pee) is derived from *Hopituh Shinumu,* meaning "the peaceful people." These Indians are small of stature, with high cheekbones, straight broad noses, slanting and large eyes, reddish-brown skin. They have a highly developed artistic sense, and many of them are real artists, making practically every article—baskets, pottery, jewelry, blankets—made by other Indians. They are also clever in making masks and Kachina dolls. The best of these delightful figurines are works of art. Actually, the carved figure, which we call a Kachina Doll, represents the masked Kachina who appears in religious dances as an impersonator of a Kachina spirit. Thus the term "kachina" refers to a number of things closely associated in the religious rites of the Hopi. However, a strange feature of their religion is that the home of their gods is not in the region but on the San Francisco Peaks which dominate the very distant landscape. To this day, some Hopi still make pilgrimages to these peaks for religious reasons.

Hopi Indians perform the feather dance in front of the Hopi House on the South Rim each afternoon. Fred Harvey photo.

Dry-land farming is the Hopi's occupation, although some are becoming extensive sheep raisers. All Hopi villages have the same religion, customs, and language—however, they differ somewhat in their dress and crafts. The Indians of First Mesa are skilled in the art of pottery-making. On Second Mesa, coiled basketry of a distinctive design is manufactured. On the westernmost or Third Mesa, plaques and baskets of wicker are a specialty.

The Hopi is monogamous, a man has but one wife. Divorce is easy—the woman owns the house and when she is through with a man she simply puts his saddle outside the front door. The division of labor between husband and wife is natural. The wife takes care of the children, keeps the house, and prepares the food. The man works the fields, herds the sheep, and supplies the fuel. He produces the food on land owned by the wife's family or clan. Inheritance is through the female line—the clan.

The Hopis are deeply religious and their many dance ceremonies centering about the kiva are very beautiful in their ever-recurring symbolism of rain, cloud, lightning, and the growth of corn. The fame of these religious ceremonies has spread across the world. In general, the main portion of each ceremony is performed in an appropriate kiva, a rectangular underground chamber that serves as a workshop in the daytime, a fraternal lodge in the evening, and sometimes a sleeping place for men and boys. Parts of every ceremony are held in a particular kiva. The ceremony usually ends, however, with a public pageant in the pueblo plaza on the ninth day. This portion of the ceremony bears the inappropriate name of "dance." Since few are fortunate enough to witness the solemn ceremonies that precede in the kiva, it is these colorful outdoor pageants that are best known. The ceremonies largely venerate some event of importance in Hopi mythology. Prayers for prosperity and of thanksgiving are said. These prayers are usually for rain, the growth of crops, and for fertility.

The cycle of Hopi ceremonies begins in the late fall and continues monthly through the year. Below is the Third Mesa calendar. The schedules of the other two mesas show a few differences.

November—Wuwu chim, 9 days. This ceremony in which four societies take part portrays what happened in the mythical under-

152

Kabotie, the Hopi Indian artist, explains the painting of the Snake Legend in the Hopi Room of the Watchtower at Desert Point on the South Rim. Fred Harvey photo.

world before the Hopi emerged to the world above. It is the tribal initiation.

December—Soyala, 9 days. A winter solstice ceremony. Prayer offerings are made and given to friends and relatives. It is a custom similar to our giving of Christmas cards. These prayer offerings, pahos and nakwakuosis, are made of feathers fastened to hand-spun cotton string and perhaps to a little stick. There are special forms for every occasion.

January—Pamuya, 1 day. Prayer offerings are made to be used months later in the summer Snake and Flute ceremonies. "Buffalo Dance"—a social dance.

February—Powamu, 12 days. This is the "Bean Dance." Beans are planted in the kiva and the pale shoots harvested on the 12th day at which time a dance is held.

March—No formal ceremony except the manufacture of prayer offerings for future dances.

April—Kachina Dances, 1 day. In the Kachina Dances the adult Hopi dancers wear masks. They distribute presents among the group. Little girls receive the famous Kachina Dolls, and the little boys receive bows and arrows. The whole idea resembles Santa Claus and the giving of Christmas gifts, though originally the dance was—and still symbolizes—a fertility dance.

May—Kachina Dances, 1 day.

June—Kachina Dances, 1 day.

July—Niman Kachina, 9 days. The Kachinas depart for their home on the San Francisco Mountains. A sort of Götterdämmerung, Indian-style.

August—Snake and Flute Dances, 9 days.

September—Marau, 9 days. Performed by women.

October—Oagol. "Basket Dance." Performed by women. Prayers are given for health and prosperity.

The major ceremonies have certain features in common. Each is conducted by one or more chiefs whose offices are hereditary. Each has eight days of secret rites and ends with a public dance on the ninth day. All ceremonies include the same techniques: offering prayer sticks, building an altar of sacred objects, sprinkling medicine, prayer, song, and dance.

The August Snake Dance draws a large number of visitors to the Hopi towns. The snake ceremonies, an elaborate prayer for rain and corn, extend over a nine-day period and involve a complicated ritual. The significance of much of it seems to be forgotten.

On the first day of the nine-day period the priests of the Antelope and the Snake fraternities, or clan, enter their respective kivas and hang up the natsi, a bunch of feathers which, on the fifth day, is replaced by a bow decorated with eagle feathers. They manufacture prayer sticks. On the second, third, fourth and fifth days, the snake men conduct ceremonial hunts for snakes. On the sixth, seventh, and eighth days, at the time of the setting of the morning star, just before dawn, in the Antelope Kiva, the symbolic marriage of Tiyo and the snake maiden takes place, followed by the singing of sixteen traditional songs. In the afternoon of the eighth day a public pageant occurs, in which the antelope and the snake priests take part. This pageant summarizes in miniature the Snake Dance to occur on the next day, with ears of corn used instead of live snakes. On the ninth day at dawn youths race from the cornfields near the encampment to the top of the mesa. By noon the snakes are prepared and in the late afternoon the Snake Dance completes the series of ceremonies.

The Hopi do not worship or make their prayers directly to the snakes. The snakes are simply messengers to carry prayers to the rain gods. If the snakes are well treated by being danced over, sprinkled with sacred meal, washed with sacred water and bathed during these elaborate ceremonies, the Indians reason that the snakes will most certainly return all these courtesies by asking their friends, the rain gods, to send rain.

The snakes used in the ceremonies are, in general, of three kinds: the harmless Arizona gopher snake, sometimes called "bull snake"; the Great Basin Striped Racer, sometimes called "whip snake"; and the poisonous Prairie rattlesnake, locally called "sidewinder." The dancers are frequently bitten but seem not to suffer any serious effects. This is probably because the snakes, during their preparation for the ceremony, are continually teased and allowed to strike. From research work on the venom of the rattlesnake which was conducted some years ago at the University of Pennsylvania, it was found that after a rattlesnake had struck and discharged its venom, several days were required before the poison sacs were full again. After a snake is "milked" (allowed to strike some inanimate object) it is virtually harmless for a day or so.

155

The Hopi are friendly and very hospitable, and tourists are welcome at their various ceremonies. All spectators should remember, however, that they are guests at a religious ceremony and appropriate behavior is expected. Taking photographs or drawing pictures at a ceremony is absolutely forbidden. It is suggested that you leave your camera locked up in your car.

Third Mesa villages (Hotevilla, Bacobi, Oraibi, and Kiakochomovi) are approximately 135 miles from Grand Canyon Village via Arizona State Routes 64 and 264. The distance between First Mesa and Third Mesa is about 25 miles. The villages of the easternmost or First Mesa are Hano, Suhomovi, Walpi and Polacca, while Mishnonghovi, Shipolovi, Toreva and Shongopovi are important villages of the Second Mesa.

Reservation gas stations are usually open from 8 A.M. to 6 P.M. Since the Hopi villages have few stores, tourists should carry water and food during an all-day visit. (Overnight accommodations are available at Keams Canyon which is on the reservation.) Sunglasses and hats are advisable for protection from the summer sun, and camp stools may be useful during the long waits between dances. In winter or early spring, warm attire is needed for protection from the cold wind blowing across the mesas.

THE NAVAJO

The Navajos are the largest of all the Indian tribes in the United States (over 85,000 persons), and their reservation is the largest in America, covering some 22,589 square miles, including a large part of the Painted Desert. They prefer, however, to live in the open or in isolated hogan homes made of logs and adobe rather than in villages. They are semi-nomadic, moving with their sheep and goats from winter to summer hogans and doing some farming.

When the Spaniards visited the Southwest, in 1540, the Navajos were an agricultural people. They had large patches of land under cultivation—they even practiced the art of irrigation. After the Spaniards introduced sheep it was not long until they were extensive sheep raisers. While the women tended sheep and the crops, the men hunted and fought. For nearly three hundred years the Navajos roamed the Southwest, preying on other tribes. So menacing were they toward the westward-moving white man that in 1863 Kit Carson, acting under Government orders, herded them together and moved them to

New Mexico where they were held in captivity at Fort Sumner. In 1868, after being starved into submission, they were allowed to return to their homeland in Arizona and once more roamed the sagebrush plains.

Today they are stock raisers, owning thousands of cattle and horses. Their sheep and goats number over a million. Their very existence depends upon their flocks. They eat the flesh, drink the milk. Wool makes the blankets from which they derive half a million dollars each year. Surplus wool is sold or traded for coffee, sugar, and bright fabrics. Rug weaving and silversmithing are the outstanding arts of the Navajos. Pottery and baskets once made by them are created now by only a few potters and basket weavers and they are used entirely for ceremonial purposes.

The Navajo women are the weavers. They tend the sheep, card the wool, spin and weave it. The Spaniards in 1540 found the Navajo loom just as complete as it is today and the art of weaving in a well-advanced stage. In making a rug a set pattern is never followed, the weaver making up the pattern as she weaves. This is the reason no two rugs are ever exactly alike.

The Navajo men are the silversmiths, making beautiful jewelry which is set with turquoise. Before the coming of the Spaniards, jewelry was made of stones, shells, and bones. The Navajos suffered a severe shock when the Spaniards appeared wearing ornaments of silver, copper, and tin, which glittered in the sun. It was not long before they acquired metal, and silver has never lost its charm for these people. As a matter of fact, the possession and display of jewelry is a significant measure of the individual's wealth; consequently quantities of "hard goods" may deck the satin skirts and velvet blouses of the women or the store-bought shirts and levis of the men.

The Navajo is polygamous, although the government tries to discourage the practice. Personal property is individually owned and consists of silver and turquoise, which he calls hard goods; of textiles and hides, which he calls soft goods; and stock, such as goats, cattle, and horses. Such intangible things as songs, chants, and formulae for divination, he also considers as personal property. Inheritance follows the maternal line—the clan. The father's wealth will not pass to his children but will be inherited by his sister's children.

Navajo ceremonies are nearly always curing ceremonies or medicine chants. One man out of every eight in the Navajo tribe is a medicine man. If they are good medicine men, they are superior

157

beings, doctors, religious leaders, and historians. They must learn the chants passed down from generation to generation for different kinds of illnesses, and they must also master the art of sand painting, which is an important part of the healing ceremony.

Sand paintings are very elaborate pictures made with five to nine different colors of sand. These are made on the ground or floor of the hogans. Sand painters must memorize the complicated pictures which depict some part of their mythology. No originality is used in this art, each painting being a pattern handed down from generation to generation. The medicine men are trained in letting the sand trickle between the first two fingers and thumb, paintings being made without error.

An old legend states that the first Indian taught the art of sand painting had revealed to him pictures painted on the clouds. The divine beings did not trust the people of the earth with permanent pictures. Ancient Indians thus believed that pictures should be destroyed the same day as made—therefore, sand was used. To this day Navajos consider it very bad luck to make a permanent copy of sand paintings.

Actually, the religion of the Navajo is quite different from that of the Hopi. In general, the Hopi prays to beneficent spirits to help him in his troubles; while the Navajo, in general, exercises his religion to drive out evil spirits. The Hopi prays to the Kachinas to bring rain; the Navajo exorcises devils. If a person has bad dreams, or is ill, there is a devil that must be driven away, and elaborate ceremonies, presided over by a medicine man, are held as the patient demands. The best known of the Navajo ceremonies are the Mountain Chants, the Night Chants of the Yeibichai, the Devil Chasing Chants, and the War or Squaw Dance.

The Mountain Chants, sometimes called the Fire Dance, is a nine-day ceremony, consisting of four days of purification, four days of sand paintings, and the last day the Fire Dance. Fires are made in a circle enclosing a large corral-like space in the center of which is built a larger fire. Here dancers, coated with white clay, gather. They dance in and out among the fires with feather wands. They dance through the entire night. The Navajos believe that as long as the dancer sings the fire song he will not be burned. The Mountain Chants usually take place in the late fall and winter.

The Night Chants of the Yeibichai, also an elaborate nine-day ceremony, are prayers to the Yei, the ancient original gods who seem

Navajo craftsmen at work: jewelry making (above) and weaving (below). In the latter, the weaver spins yarn to be used in the rug on the loom behind her. This method of spinning on the hand-twirled spindle has been common to peoples all over the world for centuries, and the loom is a type that was in use before America was discovered. Bureau of Indian Affairs photos.

to be like the Hopi Kachinas. The ceremony centers around the patient who lies in the hogan during this time. Near dusk on the last day many Indians gather from far and wide—a great fire is made, around which the dance takes place.

The Devil Chasing Chants, which may be held at any time, are composed to drive the illness directly out of a patient's body.

The War Dance, better known as the Squaw Dance, is a two-day ceremony held in the summer and early fall. Although it was originally designed to drive away ghosts from warriors who had been out on scalping expeditions, it is used today to drive away bad dreams, to drive out devils from some ill person, and as a social function. It is the one chance that young people have to meet persons of the opposite sex of other clans. It is here that courting often begins.

At the present time there are about fifty clans among the Navajos —they have made for themselves a seventy-five member council— which deals with government representatives in all matters pertaining to the whole tribe. The council are elected by people from the various parts of the reservation. The center of Navajo activity is at their one big agency at Window Rock, Arizona.

Properly to view the Navajo people, one must roam their reservation, for they have never gathered in communities—but still keep the ways of their fathers, living a nomadic life. Most of the trip from South Rim to North Rim (see page 59) is made through the Navajo Reservation. The Trading Posts at Gray Mountain, Cameron, The Gap, and Tuba City provide fascinating sights in Navajo country.

THE PAIUTE AND HUALAPAI

Paiute Indians occupy the Kaibab Reservation in the northwest part of Arizona along the Utah border. Because traditionally these desert Indians maintained a gathering culture, digging for all edible roots, they became known as the "Digger Tribe." Today, most Paiutes speak English, live and dress like the white man, and engage in cattle raising and wage work as their major sources of income. Their basketry is well made and follows traditional designs. Paiute tribal offices are at Moccasin, Arizona. The governing body is a tribal council of six members, elected to hold office for three years.

About one-fourth of the Hualapai Reservation is a jumble of gorges, cliffs, and inaccessible mesas, a western continuation of the Grand Canyon. The remainder is mostly rolling hills and mesas. Stock raising is the chief means of livelihood among the Hualapais. Three livestock associations have been formed, and a tribal herd is maintained. Some income is also derived from timber sales, business leases, and grazing fees. All tribal income except that allocated to specific enterprises goes into a general fund for reservation improvement, tribal loans, and relief. The people govern themselves through an elective nine-member council. Most of their native crafts are gone except for their traditional styled baskets which are well made.

U.S. Route 66 to the Grand Canyon and other scenic attractions to the east passes through the Hualapai Reservation, and towns located on the highway benefit from tourism. Peach Springs is the headquarters of the Hualapai Tribal Council.

NATIONAL MONUMENTS

If you are interested in early Indian culture, there are three National Monuments close to Grand Canyon National Park that are very worthwhile and you should make every effort to visit them.

WUPATKI AND SUNSET CRATER NATIONAL MONUMENTS

In 1065 A.D., the few Indians living at and near what is now Sunset Crater National Monuments were startled by the outbreak of a volcanic eruption. As the sky became overcast with volcanic ash, and as cinders started covering their homes and farms, they hurried away. (Timbers taken from the houses of these people—excavated from the cinders and ash—have furnished the evidence by which this geologically recent eruption has been dated.) When the eruption ceased, a new cinder cone 1,000 feet high had been built, with jagged lava flows at its base. Black volcanic ash covered an area 800 square miles surrounding the cone. This volcanic ash, acting as a mulch, transformed the soil into excellent farmland. And this, in turn, drew the farming Indians back into the area. The ruins of this post-eruption civilization are now preserved in Wupatki National Monument. The remains of the volcano—the cinder cone and lava beds—are preserved as Sunset Crater National Monument.

About 600 A.D., a few farming Indians had lived in the area near the San Francisco Peaks. These Indians lived in pit houses—

roofed pits—which were very efficient dwellings in this climate because they could easily keep heat in or out, whichever was needed. Because of the lack of moisture in the soil, only the few very best areas could be used for growing crops, and as a result the community remained small. But there is evidence that some people were living here at the time of the volcanic eruption of 1065.

The Indians soon discovered in the post-eruption period that corn could be raised in areas where plants previously had shriveled and died from lack of water. Word of this newly excellent farmland filtered out over the Southwest and Indians from all over the region moved there.

The area became a melting pot of cultures. Indian families came from all directions. The Pueblo dry farmer from eastern and northern Arizona mingled here with the Hohokam irrigation farmer from southern Arizona. This is the only place at which evidences of this mingling have been found. Influences from the Mogollon groups to the south and east and the Cohonino groups to the west have also been discovered here.

Each tribe came with corn seed and digging sticks to cultivate the cinder soils. As the tribes met and mingled, the differences between them became less and less apparent.

The people developed villages throughout the cinder-covered area. One of the most important and longest inhabited of these was one now called Wupatki, a Hopi word for "Tall House." Its location and size were probably determined by the presence of a spring, one of the few in this region. From an insignificant pueblo of a few rooms, Wupatki grew until it became the largest in the region. During the 1100's, it contained more than 100 rooms, was in places at least three stories high, and had a population of 250 to 300 persons.

To one side of the Wupatki Ruin, protected from the prevailing winds, was an open-air amphitheater which possibly was used for public ceremonies. In the valley below was a ball court of stone masonry, one of two found in the vicinity. Little is known of the game that was played there. Remains of ball courts found in southern Arizona have been dated to the period before 1150, and the idea was probably brought to Wupatki by migrants from that region.

During the 1200's people started leaving the area, and by 1300 no one remained. They left mainly because the cinders had been stripped from the soil by the winds that had originally spread them there and the droughts, ending with the great drought of 1276-99.

Wupatki National Monument. "Wupatki" means "long house" in the Hopi language. Most important ruin in the San Francisco Mountain region, it was occupied longer than other ruins of the region. Various rooms date between 1087 and 1197 A.D. Abandonment took place around 1250 A.D. Extreme dryness of climate and excellent drainage have preserved wood, textiles, and other perishable materials to an unusual extent. National Park Service photo.

Aside from the trees and other plants that have gained a foothold amid the cinders and lava, Sunset Crater probably appears much as it did soon after the eruption. Remains of the hot springs, spatter cones, and other evidences of volcanism look as if they had barely had time to cool. Black cinder dunes, large cinder fields, and the twisted, gnarled, and jagged "slag heaps" of the lava flows create an atmosphere of strangeness.

A small lava cave, near the foot of the cone, contains ice the year around. You are asked not to remove any of the ice, because removal would raise the temperature of the cave during the summer and cause the remaining ice to disappear. Consider those who will be later visitors.

An easy trail crosses some of the lava flow, past the lava cave and other intriguing features. The "Lava Flow Nature Trail" guidebook, available at the register stand, is keyed to numbers posted along the trail.

Another trail leads to the crater rim, at 8,000 feet. Difficult of access because of the loose cinders, the summit rewards the climber with a fine view of the unbreached crater, 400 feet deep and a quarter of a mile wide, and of the craters, lava flows, and forests of the San Francisco Peaks. To the northeast extends the colorful Painted Desert.

Wupatki National Monument contains approximately 800 Indian ruins. Wupatki Ruin itself is one of the most impressive pueblos in northern Arizona. Its walls rise from a sandstone spur at the base of a black lava mesa that overlooks the Painted Desert, with the ball court and amphitheater below the ruin.

Around Citadel Ruin is another concentration of early Indian ruins. Within a square mile there are more than 100 sites, from small earth lodges to large pueblos. The Citadel itself, as yet unexcavated, appears to have been a fortified, multi-family dwelling—probably 1 or 2 stories high and containing about 50 rooms. Just below it is the small pueblo ruin now called Nalakihu, a Hopi word for "house standing alone." Other outstanding sites in the Monument are Lomaki and Wukoki Ruins, several fortified, multi-family dwellings, and the less accessible Crack-in-the-Rock Ruin near the Little Colorado River. To visit Crack-in-the-Rock, you must make arrangements with the superintendent, whose office is near Wupatki Ruin. There are self-guiding trails to Citadel-Nalakihu and to Wupatki Ruins. Guidebooks keyed to numbers along the trails are available at the beginning of each.

Reaching the Monuments. The paved entrance roads to both Monuments lead eastward from U.S. Route 89. The Wupatki road is about 80 miles from Grand Canyon Village via Arizona State Route 64 and U.S. 89, and the Sunset Crater road is about 9 miles farther south. Thus, it is possible to reach both monuments on paved roads by driving into each from U.S. 89. The two Monuments, however, are connected by a road that will take you through 18 miles of cinder-covered hills, along the edge of the Painted Desert, and through several unusual plant and animal communities. You should stay strictly on the road, for attempting to drive on the cinders is dangerous.

Uniformed personnel are on duty the year around at Wupatki, and from May to October at Sunset Crater. Roads into Sunset Crater are sometimes closed by snow in winter. The Information Station at Sunset Crater is 4 miles from U.S. 89, Wupatki Ruin and the Visitor Center of Wupatki National Monument are 14 miles from the highway. There are no overnight facilities at either Monument. Drinking water is available at headquarters of Wupatki only.

Wupatki National Monument, containing 56 square miles, was established on December 9, 1924. Sunset Crater National Monument, containing 4½ square miles, was established on May 26, 1930. Both Monuments were established by Presidential proclamation. Elevation at Wupatki headquarters is 4,900 feet; at Sunset Crater, it is 7,000 feet. A superintendent, whose address is Wupatki National Monument, Tuba Star Route, Flagstaff, Arizona 86003, is in immediate charge of both.

WALNUT CANYON NATIONAL MONUMENT

After the eruptions of Sunset Crater, the Sinagua Indians moved into volcanic rich farmland south of the volcano. At Walnut Canyon, the Sinagua put to use one of their new crafts: masonry. The upper walls of the 400-foot-deep canyon are of limestone, with layers of different degrees of hardness. The softer layers have eroded faster than the harder layers, thus forming long but shallow cavelike recesses. The Sinagua saw that by building front walls and room and house partitions in the recesses they could have snug homes that were protected against the weather and possibly against man. They built them. More than 300 small cliff rooms fill the shadowy recesses in the canyon walls. But Walnut Canyon offered the Sinagua more

than cozy homesites. A dependable supply of water flowed along the streambed on the floor of the canyon. Fertile volcanic-cinder soil lay within about 2 miles of the canyon rim. A great variety of trees, for fuel and implements, grew within the canyon and on the mesa. Other wild plants, a source of food and medicines, lined the banks of the stream and blanketed the slopes. Game, furred and feathered, haunted canyon and mesa top. Thus the Sinagua lived in Walnut Canyon for almost 200 years. Then they abandoned their homes. Why? No one knows. Perhaps it was drought, wornout soil, pressure from enemy groups, disease—any, all, or none of these. Anthropologists believe that some of their descendants live today among the Pueblo Indians.

For 600 years, the little cliff dwellings apparently stood deserted and undisturbed. Then the white man came. During the time from the earliest known report in 1883 until the area was placed under the protection of the National Park Service in 1933, vandals removed much of the cultural material that had been left by the Sinagua, even damaging and defacing the dwellings themselves. Present understanding of the area is largely derived from investigations at contemporary sites. But you can still transport yourself back in time to the days when the Sinagua lived their lives in this lovely canyon. Their homes are here, and you can walk among them. A paved foot trail leads to 25 of the cliff dwellings rooms; from the trail, you can see 100 others.

The entrance road to Walnut Canyon National Monument is an oiled highway 3 miles long, connecting with U.S. 66 at a point 7½ miles east of Flagstaff. (Flagstaff is about 108 miles from Grand Canyon Village via Arizona State Route 64 and U.S. Route 89, or approximately 90 miles via U.S. Routes 180 and 66.) Two secondary approaches by graveled road are open in good weather. One, from the west, leaves U.S. 66 at a point 4½ miles east of Flagstaff and is 6 miles long. The other, from the east and 4 miles long, leaves U.S. 66 about 11 miles east of Flagstaff. These graveled roads make a dry-weather loop route which adds only 3½ miles to the trip for visitors traveling east or west on U.S. 66.

At Walnut Canyon National Monument ruins of small cliff dwellings built of adobe and stone are distributed under ledges of both walls of canyon. Each one-room unit apparently sheltered one family. There are no doorways in the dividing partitions. National Park Service photo.

The Monument is open all year. From May 30 through Labor Day, visiting hours are from 7 A.M. to 7 P.M. daily; for the rest of the year, from 8 A.M. to 5 P.M. The admission fee is waived for children under twelve years of age and for organized educational groups.

Your first stop in the Monument should be at the new Visitor Center. After studying the exhibits in the museum here, you will have a better understanding of what you will see in the Canyon. Employees of the National Park Service will be eager to answer your questions about the Monument and suggest ways by which you can make your visit most enjoyable and meaningful.

The trail that leads among the cliff dwellings is three-fourths of a mile long, round trip, and involves a climb of 185 feet. Elevation at the canyon rim is about 7,000 feet. The combination of the climb and the elevation will throw unaccustomed demands on your heart; and so if you have a heart condition or are uneasy about attempting the climb, you should not take the trail trip. Much can be seen from the rim of the canyon.

Accommodations are not available within the Monument. Meals and lodging may be obtained at nearby towns and along the major highways. A superintendent, whose address is Route 1, Box 790, Flagstaff, Arizona 86001, is in immediate charge of the Monument, which contains some 1,879 acres and was established on November 30, 1915.

Chapter 8.

Accommodations and Services
in the Park

ALL concession units in the Park for the accommodation of the public, such as hotels, lodges, stores, restaurants, banks, etc., are operated under contract with the United States Government. Reservations for rented accommodations should be made as far in advance as possible with Fred Harvey Reservation Office, Grand Canyon, Arizona 86023, or at 530 West 6th Street, Los Angeles, California 90014, or 80 East Jackson Boulevard, Chicago, Illinois 60604, for the South Rim; and with the Utah Parks Company, Cedar City, Utah 84720, for the North Rim. All rates have been omitted in this chapter, since they are subject to occasional change. But, remember the rates of Park concessioners are subject to National Park Service approval.

SOUTH RIM

Grand Canyon Village, a picturesque community on the South Rim, offers facilities for a brief or extended visit to Grand Canyon National Park at any time of the year. El Tovar Hotel, Bright Angel Lodge and Cabins, Grand Canyon Auto Cabins, Yavapai Lodge and the Grand Canyon Trailer Village provide accommodations for every taste and purse. Public campgrounds maintained by the National Park Service are available for the free use of motorists who bring their own camping equipment (see page 176).

El Tovar Hotel. This is one of the most famous resort hotels in America. The spacious structure with its rambling wings and broad

porches is built of native boulders and rustic pine logs; its rooms have been recently completely modernized. For more than half a century it has stood in picturesque silhouette against the Canyon Rim. It is renowned for its unobtrusive hospitality and excellent cuisine. Rooms open all year; dining room, gift shop, and cocktail lounge open May 1 to October 31.

Bright Angel Lodge and Cabins. The rambling Bright Angel Lodge and Cabins form a picturesque little village on the brink of the Canyon. The various buildings—main lodge, guest lodges, and individual cabins—are of log and stone construction, combining rustic simplicity with modern convenience. The guest lodges and numerous individual cabins of one to four rooms offer a wide choice of comfortable, moderately priced living accommodations. Open all year, including the dining room, cocktail lounge, gift shop, and coffee shop.

Grand Canyon Auto Cabins. These offer comfortably furnished sleeping and housekeeping accommodations for motorists, close to the South Rim. Public showers; maid service; firewood and water furnished. Newsstand and gift shop at Main Lodge as well as a fine cafeteria. Open a week before Easter to mid-October.

Yavapai Lodge. This comfortable motel, near the Visitor's Center, adds a number of up-to-date accommodations to those available at the South Rim. Its ten rambling structures of sixteen units each are located amidst a fragrant forest of pine and juniper. Ample parking facilities are adjacent to each unit. All rooms have two double beds, dressing room space, and combination bath. Open a week before Easter to October 31. (Both the Auto Cabins and Yavapai Lodge are so constructed that they can be opened to the public within 12 hours when needed during the winter months, and during the Thanksgiving and Christmas seasons they are open.)

Phantom Ranch. Nesting at the very bottom of the Canyon among the towering crags of Bright Angel Canyon—nearly a vertical mile

---

El Tovar Hotel as seen from the Bright Angel Lodge. Fred Harvey photo.

below the Rim—the Ranch comprises a group of rustic cabins and a central lodge surrounding a swimming pool filled with crystal-clear water. Inner-canyon trails are the only means of reaching this secluded place (see photograph, page 81). Open all year.

NORTH RIM

There are two accommodation facilities available on the North Rim of the Park. They are:

Grand Canyon Lodge and Cabins. The handsome central Lodge rises from the very brink of the chasm, supported by huge flying buttresses which are continuations of the natural stone pillars eroded from the face of the cliff. Constructed of native sandstone and rough-hewn ponderosa pine timbers from the Kaibab Forest, it harmonizes perfectly with its sublime surroundings. The building contains a recreation room, lounge, dining room, cocktail lounge, curio store, and coffee shop. The guest cabins and lodges spread out from near the Main Lodge. Open about June 15 through breakfast the day after Labor Day.

North Rim Inn. The accommodations here are comfortably furnished cabins. In the Inn building, there is a fine cafeteria. Open about May 15 through second weekend in October.

CAMPGROUNDS

There are two basic types of campgrounds available in Grand Canyon National Park. The improved campground is an organized layout having well-defined roads, parking spaces, and campsites. Drinking water and sanitary facilities, including toilets and refuse cans, are furnished on a community basis. Each campground has a designed capacity based on the number of campsites therein. A campground site, or campsite, is a clearly marked plot or location within a campground which provides accommodations for camping by an individual, family, or party. A typical campsite in a campground would include a parking space, fireplace, table and bench combination, and a tent space; however, in a walk-in campground or walk-in section of a campground, the parking space is provided but not as an integral part of each campsite.

172

Yavapai Lodge contains modern motel-type accommodations. Fred Harvey photo.

There are three improved camp and trailer grounds inside the Park. Camping and house trailer parking is free in all campgrounds. House trailers are permitted in designated sites in all campgrounds but there are no utility or sewer hookups in the campgrounds. (All camping sites are on a first-come, first-served basis—*none may be reserved.* We suggest an early afternoon arrival to assure adequate camping space.) There is, however, on the South Rim, the concessioner-operated Grand Canyon Trailer Village, east of Mather campground, whose 193 modern sites have water, sewer, and power hookups.

173

A charge is made per day or per week. Open all year; from May 1 to October 31. Stay is limited to 15 days. Nearby is the Camper's Service Building which offers public showers, snack bar, ice, and laundromat service (closed from mid-October to mid-April). Reservations in Trailer Village are advisable and are available from Fred Harvey (see page 169).

Mather Campground

Location: South Rim, Grand Canyon Village. (Forested Area.) Open all year. 328 campsites with tables, benches, and firegrates.

7 group sites with two tables, benches, and firegrates at each site.

Water: Piped water at convenient locations.

Rest rooms: Flush-type.

There is a free sanitary disposal station for trailers near the Trailer Village entrance.

Camper Service Building with laundromat, showers, ice, and snack bar. (Concessioner operated. Open summer months approximately mid-April to mid-October.)

General Store at Grand Canyon Village with groceries and campers' supplies. (Open weekdays all year; open Sundays and holidays during the summer.)

Wood vending machine near the campgrounds, or wood may be purchased at General Store.

Park ranger is stationed at campground entrance from first week in June through Labor Day.

Desert View Campground

Location: South Rim, near East Entrance Station (Highway 64 from Cameron). Open about May 1 to October 1. (Forested Area.)

50 campsites with tables, benches, and firegrates.

Water: Piped water at convenient locations.

Rest rooms: Pit-type.

No utility hookups or disposal station for trailers.

Snack bar and souvenirs at Trading Post. (Open 8 A.M. to 5 P.M. all year.)

A general store with camper provisions is located adjacent to the campground.

Large chunks of wood are provided—carry small axe or saw.

174

The famous "sing-away" for departing guests in front of the Grand Canyon Lodge on the North Rim. Union Pacific Railroad photo.

North Rim (Bright Angel) Campground

Location: North Rim (Highway 67). (Forested Area.) Elevation 8,153 feet. (Open mid-May to about October 1.)

78 campsites with tables, benches, and firegrates.

Water: Piped water at convenient locations.

Rest rooms: Flush-type.

Group camping area with limited number of tables and firegrates.

No trailer utility hookups or sanitary disposal on North Rim.

(Continued)

Large chunks of firewood provided—carry small axe or saw.
Pay showers and ice (block or cube) available.
Store with groceries and limited campers' supplies.

At North Rim and Mather Campgrounds arrangements can be made for organized group camping such as Boy Scouts, school groups, or other large parties. Since these arrangements require advanced planning, reservations are mandatory for large groups. Request should be sent as much in advance of the trip as possible. Write to the Superintendent, Grand Canyon National Park, Grand Canyon, Arizona 86023.

BACKCOUNTRY CAMPGROUNDS

The second type of campground is the primitive or backcountry camp. These camping areas may be accessible by either trail or road. Facilities provided are *minimum*. Each camping area has an assigned, as differentiated from designed, capacity based on the number of camping spaces therein. Superintendents assign to each camping area a capacity figure, in terms of camping spaces, based on a realistic evaluation of acreage involved, topography, and facilities provided. A fire permit is required for the use of the following primitive locations:

	No. Sites	*Sites along* *Bright Angel Trail*	No. Sites
Cottonwood	10	2.6 Mile	1
Havasu	12	4.0 Mile	1
Indian Gardens	10	5.5 Mile (Ribbon Falls)	1
		Bright Angel Creek	10

There are a number of improved campsites available in Kaibab National Forest, which almost surrounds Grand Canyon National Park. The closest ones to the Park are:

Campground	*No. of Sites*	*Location*
De Motte	20	Off Route 67, near North Entrance of Grand Canyon National Park
Jacob Lake	48	Off Route 87A, at Jacob Lake
10-X	70	Off Route 180, near South Entrance of Grand Canyon National Park

For more information on these campgrounds, write the Forest Supervisor, Kaibab National Forest, Williams, Arizona 86046. A fee is charged at Forest Campground in National Forest.

GENERAL RULES FOR GRAND CANYON CAMPGROUNDS

Camp at designated sites only. (Do not move rocks or park off pavement.) To establish occupancy, leave something at the campsite or register, when requested. But, camping or parking cars overnight along roadsides or at other undesignated spots is not permitted.

Campers must keep their campsites clean. Combustible rubbish should be burned in campfires, and all other garbage and refuse of all kinds should be placed in receptacles provided for the purpose. The drainage or dumping of refuse from any trailer, except in places or receptacles provided for such purpose is prohibited. All campers must carry their waste water to the nearest rest room for disposal. Because of the thin topsoil, heavy campground use, and the proximity of flies and rodents, no dishwater or other waste water may be drained or dumped on the ground. The cleaning of dishes or the washing of clothing at campground hydrants or in comfort stations is prohibited. Garbage, papers, or refuse of any kind should not be thrown or left on or along roads, in camping or picnic areas, or on any other Park land. Do not waste water, as it has to be pumped up from the Inner Canyon.

Quiet is maintained between the hours of 10 P.M. and 6 A.M. The operation of motor-driven power generators or similar noise-producing motors or machinery is prohibited. The installation of permanent camping facilities by visitors is also prohibited. Campers should not leave their camps unattended for more than 48 hours without special permission of the ranger-in-charge, obtained in advance. Camping is limited to 14 days.

Dogs and cats are allowed in the Park if they are on leashes or otherwise under physical restrictive control, but not on trails under any circumstances.

In the improved campgrounds, wood-gathering is prohibited. Leave deadwood where it has fallen and help preserve the natural scene. At Mather Campground, wood is available from a vending machine or may be purchased at the General Store. Large chunks of firewood

177

are provided at North Rim and Desert View Campgrounds. At primitive campgrounds, take only fallen dead trees for firewood. As previously stated, campfire permits are required for building fires in primitive campgrounds or in areas outside designated campgrounds. The reason for this is obvious. The rangers must know where such fires are being built, since they maintain a constant watch over forests of the Park and are on twenty-four-hour fire-call duty.

In public campgrounds the regular fireplaces constructed for the convenience of visitors must be used. Gas stoves may be used on tables or clear ground. Be sure your campfire is out before you leave it. There should not be one spark visible. Feel the wet ashes and be sure they are cold before you leave. Be equally careful with your cigarettes. Just one cigarette or match, carelessly thrown, can destroy a whole forest. All kinds of fireworks are prohibited.

As in all National Parks, do not feed, touch, tease, or molest any native bird, animal, or reptile.

All these campground regulations are enforced for your benefit.

PICNIC FACILITIES

Picnic sites are located at intervals along all paved Park roads (see Chapter 3). At these areas, no water is available, and no camping or fires permitted except for the Village Picnic Area site near the Auto Lodge and Cafeteria. This major picnic site has the following features:

75 sites with tables, benches, firegrates, and a few charcoal grills.
Water: Piped water at convenient locations.
Rest rooms: Flush-type.
General Store in Grand Canyon Village with groceries and campers' supplies. (Open weekdays all year; open Sundays and holidays during the summer.)
Wood available at General Store. No camping is permitted.

ACTIVITIES AND SERVICES

Almost every possible tourist service is available to visitors of the Park. Recreational activities are varied, but in keeping with the natural surrounding. The activities and services that are available on both Rims are as follows:

178

Two of the major gift shops on the South Rim: The Lookout Studio (top) and Hopi House (bottom). Fred Harvey photo.

Mail Service

South Rim. Visitors should have their mail sent to them in care of General Delivery, Grand Canyon, Arizona 86023, and it may be picked up at the post office in the village. Those stopping at hotels or lodges may have their mail sent in care of Fred Harvey, Grand Canyon, Arizona 86023, with the name of the accommodation where they have reservations. Postal drops are at the front desk of the hotel, lodges, and cabin headquarters.

North Rim. Mail for persons traveling to the North Rim should be addressed as follows: General Delivery, Grand Canyon North Rim, Arizona 86022. The post office is located at the Lodge. Of course, if you are staying at the Grand Canyon Lodge your mail can be addressed in care of it.

Telegraph and Telephone

South and North Rim. Telegrams may be sent from the front desks of inns, lodges, and hotels to any part of the world during daytime hours. You should use Grand Canyon National Park, Arizona, as your telegraphic address, and inquire for messages at the main office in Grand Canyon Village (South Rim) and Grand Canyon Lodge (North Rim).

Notices of undelivered telegrams and urgent messages are posted daily on bulletin boards at Ranger Stations, Visitor Centers, Entrance Stations, and elsewhere throughout the Park.

Long-distance and local (intra-park) telephone calls may be made from booths located throughout the Park.

Medical Service

South Rim. A well-equipped Grand Canyon Hospital, with staff physicians and nursing staff, is located in Grand Canyon Village. Physicians on the hospital staff are on call for emergency medical attention at any point on the South Rim. Fees for hospital, medical, and ambulance services are approved by the National Park Service and are in keeping with standard charges throughout the country.

North Rim. A nurse is on duty at the Grand Canyon Lodge office. First aid also may be obtained on both Rims from Ranger Stations and Visitor Centers in case of emergency.

Religious Services

South Rim. Protestant Sunday services and Sunday school are held in the Community Building and in the Visitor Center Amphitheater, while the Latter-Day Saints hold their services at the high school. Roman Catholic Sunday services are held in the lounge of the Bright Angel Lodge. During the summer, sunrise services are held at the "Shrine of the Ages" on the Rim. Check bulletin boards throughout the South Rim for times of the services.

North Rim. Protestant, Roman Catholic, and Latter-Day Saints services are held on Sundays at the Grand Canyon Lodge. Check bulletin board at the Lodge, Inn, and campgrounds for details.

Garages, Service Stations

For automobile repairs, public service garages are located in the Park on both Rims. Gasoline service stations are found on South Rim near the Visitor Center and Desert View (in summer only). On North Rim, a service station is available near North Rim Inn.

Stores and Newsstands

South Rim. Babbitt Brothers Trading Company, carrying groceries and drug supplies, clothing, sportswear, hardware, and other items, is located in Grand Canyon Village and also a small store similarly stocked is located at Desert View. There is also a soda fountain at the Trading Company's village store. Curios are available at the Trading Post at Desert View.

The newsstands in El Tovar Hotel, Bright Angel Lodge, and Grand Canyon Auto Cabins carry stocks of souvenirs and curios, in addition to current publications.

North Rim. Curios, current publications, fountain service, and travelers' supplies at both Grand Canyon Lodge and North Rim Inn. Groceries are available at the North Rim store.

Curio, Gift, and Souvenir Shops

South Rim. At or near Grand Canyon Village, photographic supplies, post cards, curios, slides, souvenirs are available at the Bright Angel Lodge, El Tovar Hotel, Kolb Studio, Verkamps Store, Hopi House, Lookout Studio, and the Auto Lodge. At Hermit's Rest, there is a curio shop, plus refreshments. At both the Watchtower and the Trading Post at Desert View, curios, Indian items, post cards, souvenirs, photo supplies, slides, etc., are available. At the Trading Post, there is a soda fountain luncheonette.

The Lookout Studio, in addition to being a photo and gift shop, is a quaint observatory on the edge of the South Rim near the head of the Bright Angel Trail. It is equipped with a large binocular telescope in the tower for observing the most distant reaches of the Canyon by day, and for viewing the heavens by night.

North Rim. In addition to Grand Canyon Lodge, there is a curio store located near the North Rim Inn where souvenirs, photographic supplies, slides, postcards and so on are available.

Barber Shop and Beauty Salon

A barber shop and beauty salon are both located in Bright Angel Lodge, while a barber shop can be found at the Grand Canyon Lodge on the North Rim.

Laundry

A self-service laundromat is available at the Camper Service Building at Mather Campground. Laundry and dry-cleaning service is available daily (including holidays) except Sundays at South Rim lodges and hotels; also one-day service can be had.

Ice

Ice is available at the Campers' Service Building, Auto Campers Cabins, service stations, and the Desert View Trading Post on the South Rim, and at the general store on the North Rim.

Auto Rentals

Automobiles may be rented at the Grand Canyon Airport. Chauffeur-driven five-passenger touring cars may be chartered for private

use on regular or special trips. The transportation desk at El Tovar
Hotel or the Bright Angel Lodge can give you information on this.

Motor Trips

Motor coach trips are available on both Rims. Details, page 57.

Trail Trips

Mule trips into the Inner Canyon leave both Rims daily during
the summer months. Trips to Plateau Point and Phantom Ranch
from the South Rim are made the year around. Suitable riding clothes
(slacks or dungarees and broad-brimmed hat) are necessary for all
trail trips. Apparel of this type may be rented at El Tovar Hotel
and Bright Angel Lodge. (Children under twelve years old not taken
on trail trips. Also, persons weighing over 200 pounds cannot be accommodated.) To make arrangements for care of children while
adults are on trail trips, write Manager, El Tovar Hotel, Grand
Canyon, Arizona 86023. No facilities available for the care of pets.

Saddle-horse trips are available on both Rims (see pages 59 and
68). Special guides for private saddle-horse groups are available.

Scenic Flights

Daily scenic flights—by airplane or helicopter—over the Grand
Canyon are available during the summer months from the Grand
Canyon Airport 8 miles south of Park Headquarters. Information may
be had at the airport or at El Tovar Hotel or Bright Angel Lodge
transportation desks.

Swimming

It is not advisable to go swimming in the Colorado River as it is
a very turbulent stream with undertows and dangerous rapids. The
place to swim is in the pool at Phantom Ranch. There is no charge.

Entertainment

South Rim. From June 1 through Labor Day, there is dancing
nightly (except Sunday) at the Bright Angel Lodge. Twice a week,
movies are shown in the Community House. Programs include recent
releases of feature films, newsreels, etc. Also late each afternoon the

Indian employees of Fred Harvey perform some of their colorful ceremonial dances at the Hopi House.

Illustrated talks on the Canyon's wildlife, geology, plantlife, history, etc., are given at 8 P.M. every summer evening by a Park Naturalist at the Mather Amphitheater (located behind Visitor Center), Village Amphitheater (located in Village Picnic Area), and the Desert View Campfire Circle (located in campground at Desert View). See bulletin board for schedules.

A movie and slide program (admission charged) of early Colorado River exploration by the Kolb brothers is shown twice daily at the Kolb Studio, west of Bright Angel Lodge.

North Rim. Variety programs and talent shows are given nightly at 9 P.M. (following naturalist talk) at the Grand Canyon Lodge by Utah Park Company employees. Dancing follows, except on Sunday.

Another program presented by the employees of the Lodge is the "singing away of the buses" each day. As the departing guests are ready to leave, the young men and women forsake their various duties to gather in front of the Lodge and sing an unforgettable farewell.

In addition to the naturalist illustrated talks at the Lodge, similar ones are given nightly at 8 P.M. at Campground Amphitheater.

PUBLICATIONS

These publications are handled by the Grand Canyon Natural History Association, a non-profit distributing organization designed to aid in the interpretation of the features of Grand Canyon National Park. Please include *10 cents* for postage for *each* publication ordered (except Bird Checklist and Geologic Map); please do not send stamps in payment. Address all orders to the Grand Canyon Natural History Association, Box 219, Grand Canyon, Arizona 86023. (All prices subject to change without notice.)

Prehistoric People of the Northern Southwest, Bulletin No. 12
    (The story of prehistoric man in the Grand Canyon region) $ .60
Grand Canyon—Origin and Scenery, Bulletin No. 13
    (A well-illustrated and descriptive explanation) 60
Grand Canyon Wild Flowers (Annotated checklist with key;
    illustrated in color and black-and-white pictures) 5.00

Plants of Grand Canyon National Park, Bulletin No. 10
  (Annotated checklist, with distribution) . . . . Free
Grand Canyon Birds, Field Checklist (Lists all species known
  to occur in the Park, with range and frequency of occur-
  rence) . . . . Free
Grand Canyon Amphibians and Reptiles, Field. Checklist
  of species . . . . Free
Grand Canyon-The Story Behind the Scenery, Merrill D. Beal $1.00
Ancient Landscapes of the Grand Canyon Region
  (A popular illustrated geology booklet, by Dr. E. D. McKee) .50
Exploration of the Colorado River
  (Report of the J. W. Powell Expedition, 1869) 3.75
Bible Creation Story and Grand Canyon
  (An interesting comparison by George W. Wahlin) 35

U.S. Geological Survey Topographic Maps
  Bright Angel Quadrangle 50
  Grand Canyon National Monument 1.00
Geologic Map—Bright Angel Quadrangle of Grand Canyon
  National Park (In color, with text "Geologic History of
  Bright Angel Quadrangle" on reverse) 1.50

Slide Sets of Visitor Center Dioramas
  Set No. 1 (4 slides)—A Swamp of the Permian Period;
              Reptiles of a Permian Desert; Trilobites of a
              Cambrian Sea; Discovery of the Grand Canyon 1.00
  Set No. 2 (4 slides)—Powell River Expedition, 1869; Sea
              Life of the Cambrian Period; Amphibian of a
              Permian Swamp; Eroded Lowlands of Precam-
              brian Era 1.00

GRAND CANYON PLACE NAMES

While some of the place names are purely descriptive, many are to commemorate scientists, explorers, Indian tribes, leaders of religion, mythologic and romantic personages. Aztec and Indian terms occur and the origin of a few names is unknown.

AKABA, MOUNT. Named for an Indian family who lived in the vicinity of this butte.

ALARCON TERRACE. Spanish navigator, Captain Juan Hernando de Alarcón, the first person to sail up the lower section of the Colorado River (1540-41).

ALSAP BUTTE. John T. Alsap, early Arizona pioneer.

APACHE POINT. Name of a large Indian tribe of Arizona and New Mexico region which was untiring in raiding and depredating Pueblos and whites.

APOLLO TEMPLE. The son of Jupiter and brother of Diana, God of the sun in Roman and Greek mythology.

AWATUBI CREST. Awatubi, village of the Hopi Indians on the Painted Desert, destroyed in 1770.

AYER POINT. Named for Mrs. Edward E. Ayer, first white woman known to have visited the Grand Canyon.

AZTEC AMPHITHEATER. General name for all Nahua tribes in Mexico at the time of Cortez.

BANTA POINT. Albert F. Banta, an early Arizona pioneer.

BARBENCETA BUTTE. Name of principal chief of the Navajos in 1870's, Barbenceta.

BASS CAMP. Camp owned by William W. Bass, one of the pioneer settlers of the Grand Canyon.

BEALE POINT. Army officer, Lt. Edward. F. Beale, who surveyed the first road across the Arizona Plateau.

BOUCHER CREEK. Louis D. Boucher, early resident of the Grand Canyon.

BOURKE POINT. Lt. John G. Bourke, author of several books about Arizona.

BRADLEY POINT. G. V. Bradley, member of Major Powell's 1869 expedition.

BRADY PEAK. Peter R. Brady, early Arizona settler.

BRAHMA TEMPLE. In the Hindu triad Brahma was the evolver of the universe, Vishnu the redeemer, and Siva or Shiva the destroyer.

BUDDHA TEMPLE. The title of Siddhartha, founder of Buddhism in the fifth century B.C.

CARDENAS BUTTE. Garcia Lopez de Cardenas, member of Coronado's party and leader of the first expedition of white men to see the Grand Canyon.

186

CASTOR TEMPLE. Castor and Pollux were inseparable brothers in Greek mythology.

CENTEOTL POINT. Probably an Aztec deity.

CHEMEHUEVI POINT. Named for Chemehuevi Indians, a branch of the Paiute tribe.

CHIAVRIA POINT. Juan Chiavria, a Maricopa chief.

CHEOP'S PYRAMID. An Egyptian king of the fourth dynasty, builder of the famous pyramid at Gizeh.

CHIKAPANAGI MESA. Name of Indian family.

CHUAR CREEK. Name of young Indian Chief Chur–oo–um–peak of the Kaibab tribe who worked for Major Powell.

CLEMENT POWELL BUTTE. Clement Powell, member of Major Powell's second expedition.

COCHISE BUTTE. Named for famous Apache chief.

COCOPAH POINT. A tribe of Yuma Indians living on the Colorado River.

COCONINO (PLATEAU). A name sometimes used for the Havasupai, who originally occupied much of the Arizona Plateau.

COLTER BUTTE. James G. Colter, early Arizona settler.

COMANCHE POINT. Plains Indians from farther east, whose raids were greatly feared by the Pueblos.

CONFUCIUS TEMPLE. The Chinese philosopher who taught practical morality. Lived in the fourth century B.C.

CONQUISTADOR AISLE. Spanish for conqueror. The conquistadores were especially the members of Coronado's expedition.

COPE BUTTE. Edward D. Cope, a great American naturalist specializing in fossil animals.

CORONADO BUTTE. In 1540, Francisco Vásquez de Coronado led the great Spanish expedition that discovered the Grand Canyon and penetrated as far as Kansas.

DANA BUTTE. James D. Dana, noted professor of geology at Yale for many years.

DARWIN PLATEAU. Charles R. Darwin, famous English naturalist, founder of Darwinian theory of evolution.

DEVA TEMPLE. Divine epithet, applied commonly to goddess Durga, wife of Shiva of the Hindu triad.

DE VACA TERRACE. Cabeza De Vaca, a Spanish explorer, was shipwrecked on the Gulf of Mexico coast and wandered for eight years among Indian tribes before reaching a Spanish Settlement in Mexico.

DIANA TEMPLE. Roman goddess of the moon, sister to Apollo and daughter of Jupiter.

DRUMMOND PLATEAU. Henry Drummond, a famous Scottish religious writer.

DUNN BUTTE. William H. Dunn, member of Major Powell's first expedition.

DUPPA BUTTE. B. P. Darrel Duppa, early Arizona settler.

187

DUTTON POINT. Major C. E. Dutton, United States Army, who wrote for the Government a monograph on the Grand Canyon.

ELAINE CASTLE. The Lily Maid of Astolat in Tennyson's poem, *The Idylls of the King*.

ESCALANTE BUTTE. A Spanish missionary who crossed the Arizona Plateau in 1775.

EXCALIBUR. The magical sword of King Arthur of the Round Table.

FISKE BUTTE. John Fiske, an American philosopher.

FREYA CASTLE. In Scandinavian mythology Freya is the goddess of love and womanly goodness.

GALAHAD CASTLE. The purest knight of the Round Table, a major character in *The Idylls of the King*.

GALLOWAY CANYON. Nathan Galloway, a Mormon trapper who explored the Grand Canyon.

GARCES TERRACE. A Franciscan missionary who journeyed to the Hopi Country in 1776.

GATAGAMA POINT. This is the name of an Indian family.

GAWAIN ABYSS. Gawain the courteous, one of the principal knights of the Round Table.

GEIKIE PEAK. Sir Archibald Geikie, a Scottish geologist, who for many years was director of the British Geological Survey.

GREENLAND LAKE. This lake lies on what is known as the Greenland or Walhalla Plateau.

GUINEVERE CASTLE. The wife of King Arthur of the Round Table.

GUNTHER CASTLE. The Burgundian King of the *Nibelungenlied* epic, husband of Brünhild.

HAKATAI CANYON. This is the Havasupai name for the Colorado River.

HALL BUTTE. Andrew Hall, a member of Major Powell's first expedition.

HANCE CREEK. John Hance, a local pioneer.

HANCOCK BUTTE. Captain William A. Hancock, early Arizona settler.

HATTAN TEMPLE. Andrew Hattan, member of Major Powell's second expedition.

HAVASUPAI POINT. This tribe, formerly occupying Arizona Plateau, now live in Havasu Canyon, about sixty miles from Grand Canyon Village.

HAWKINS POINT. W. R. Hawkins, member of Major Powell's first expedition.

HAYDEN, MOUNT. Charles T. Hayden, early Arizona settler.

HILLERS BUTTE. John K. Hillers, member of Major Powell's second expedition.

HOLY GRAIL TEMPLE. The cup used at the Last Supper, which the Order of the Round Table was instituted to protect.

HORUS, TEMPLE OF. In Egyptian mythology the son of Osiris and Isis, principal deities.

188

HOPI POINT. The Hopis, sometimes called the Moquis, have maintained villages overlooking the Painted Desert since long before the Spanish invasion of 1540.

HUBBELL BUTTE. Juan L. Hubbell, early Arizona settler.

HUETHEWALI, MOUNT. Indian word for observation point.

HUTTON BUTTE. Oscar Hutton, a guide to the United States Army.

HUXLEY TERRACE. Famous English biologist, Thomas H. Huxley.

ISIS TEMPLE. Principal female deity of Egypt, wife of Osiris, mother of Horus, and sometimes called "The Daughter of Ra."

IVES POINT. Lt. Joseph C. Ives, United States Army, the leader of Colorado River exploration, 1857-1858.

JEFFORDS POINT. Thomas J. Jeffords, first Indian Agent in the region.

JICARILLO POINT. An Apache Tribe of northeastern New Mexico.

JONES POINT. S. V. Jones, member of Major Powell's second expedition.

JUNO TEMPLE. Wife and sister of Jupiter, queen of Heaven in Roman mythology.

JUPITER TEMPLE. The supreme deity of the Romans.

KAIBAB (PLATEAU). Paiute word meaning "mountain-lying-down."

KIBBEY BUTTE. John H. Kibbey, early Arizona settler.

KING CREST. Clarence King was the first director of the United States Geological Survey.

KING ARTHUR CASTLE. A British chieftain of the sixth century, who, with his Knights of the Round Table, has inspired romances galore.

KRISHNA SHRINE. In Hindu mythology Krishna is the name of the eighth of the ten incarnations of the supreme god Vishnu. The ninth was in the form of Buddha; the tenth is still to come.

KWAGUNT BUTTE. Probably a Shoshonean name.

LANCELOT POINT. A Knight of the Round Table, a major character in Tennyson's poem, *The Idylls of the King.*

LE CONTE PLATEAU. Joseph LeConte was professor of geology at the University of California for over thirty years.

LIPAN POINT. An Apache tribe.

LYELL BUTTE. Sir Charles Lyell was a famous English geologist.

MANU TEMPLE. A Sanskrit word meaning "man," one of fourteen demiurgic beings (subordinate gods), each of whom presided over a period of race progressions. Manu Vaivasvata, the sun-born, is the manu of the present race of beings.

MARCOS TERRACE. Fray Marcos de Niza led the first expedition into our country from Mexico in 1539 as far as Zuni. His accounts inspired Coronado's exploration.

MARICOPA POINT. A tribe of Yuma Indians who moved from Colorado River to join the Pimas.

MARION POINT. John H. Marion, an Arizona publisher.

MARSH BUTTE. O. C. Marsh, the paleontologist.

MATKATAMIBA CANYON. Name of an Indian family.

MATTHES POINT. François E. Matthes was in charge of making a topographic map of the Grand Canyon in 1902-03 and was responsible for those eminences named for mythological deities as well as for those named for southwestern Indian tribes.

MENCIUS TEMPLE. The Latin name of the Chinese philosopher, Meng, an early Confucian.

MERLIN ABYSS. A semi-legendary character of the fifth century who figures in the Round Table legends.

MESCALERO POINT. An Apache tribe that roamed principally in New Mexico.

MIMBRENO POINT. An Apache tribe taking its name from the Mimbres Mountains of New Mexico.

MODRED ABYSS. The treacherous nephew of King Arthur, Knight of the Round Table.

MOHAVE POINT. A Yuma tribe living in vicinity of Needles.

MONTEZUMA POINT. Montezuma ruled the Aztecs at the time of the Spanish conquest. He was regarded by later Indians as a deity.

MORAN POINT. The artist, Thomas Moran, who was with Major Powell, surveying the Colorado River country in 1873.

NAJI POINT. A noted Apache warrior.

NAVAJO POINT. Nomadic Indians of the Plateau region who maintained a long warfare against Pueblos and whites.

NEWBERRY POINT. J. S. Newberry, geologist with Ives' expedition to the Canyon. Long-time professor at Columbia College, New York City.

NEWTON BUTTE. Sir Isaac Newton, famous English physicist who discovered law of gravitation.

NOVINGER BUTTE. Simon Novinger, early Arizona pioneer.

OCHOA POINT. Estavan Ochoa, early Arizona pioneer.

O'NEILL BUTTE. William "Bucky" O'Neill, Arizona pioneer and one of Roosevelt's Rough Riders.

OSIRIS. Chief Egyptian deity of good, the principle of good closely associated with Ra.

PAIUTE POINT. A name applied to many Shoshonean tribes, but perhaps belongs properly only to those living in southwestern Utah.

PANAMETA TERRACE. Named for an Indian family.

PANYA POINT. Named for an Indian family.

PAPAGO POINT. A branch tribe of Pima Indians of southern Arizona region.

PATTI BUTTE. James O. Patti, first American to see the Grand Canyon.

PAYA POINT. Lemuel Paya, a Havasupai Indian.

PIMA POINT. Popular name of tribes living in the valleys of the Gila and Salt Rivers, Arizona.

PINAL POINT. An Apache tribe.

POLLUX TEMPLE. The devoted brother of Castor, in Greek legends.

POWELL PLATEAU. Major J. W. Powell made the first expedition down the Colorado River in 1869. Subsequently Director of the United States Geological Survey and the Bureau of Ethnology.

PUTESOI CANYON. Name of an Indian family.

QUETZAL POINT. An Aztec word signifying a bird of iridescence.

RA, TOWER OF. The Egyptian sun god, a supreme deity, always victorious.

RAMA SHRINE. Hindu word for prince.

ROWE'S WELL. Stanford Rowe, early Arizona settler.

SAGITTARIUS RIDGE. A zodiac constellation visible in southern United States in the summer. Latin word signifying "Archer."

SCORPION RIDGE. One of the constellations of the zodiac.

SCYLLA BUTTE. Named after the promontory at the entrance of the Strait between Italy and Sicily, around which ancient mariners feared to go.

SET, TOWER OF. The brother or son of Osiris and his deadly enemy according to Hindu mythology.

SHALER PLATEAU. N. S. Shaler, an American geologist, long-time professor at Harvard University.

SHEBA TEMPLE. The ancient capital of the Sebaeaus in Arabia, whose queen visited Solomon.

SHINUMO CREEK. Name applied by Major Powell to the Hopi confederacy.

SHIVA TEMPLE. The avenging associate of Brahma and Vishnu in ruling the universe, now the most popular Hindu god.

SIEBER POINT. Al Sieber, early Indian scout.

SINYELLA, MOUNT. Judge Sinyella, Indian chief, born 1853, who resided on the Havasupai Indian Reservation.

SOLOMON TEMPLE. Solomon, 1033-975 B.C., son of David, King of the Jews.

SIEGFRIED'S PYRE. The hero of the great German epic, *Nibelungenlied*. The burning of his funeral pyre forms the spectacular climax of Wagner's opera, *Der Götterdämmerung*.

SPENCER TERRACE. Herbert Spencer, a distinguished English philosopher.

SULLIVAN POINT. J. W. Sullivan, early Arizona pioneer.

SUMNER BUTTE. John C. Sumner, member of Major Powell's first expedition.

TANNER TRAIL. Seth B. Tanner, a local pioneer.

THOMPSON POINT. A. H. Thompson, brother-in-law of Major Powell, who accompanied him on his famous boat trip down the Canyon.

THOR TEMPLE. Second principal Norse deity, god of thunder, son of Odin, the supreme being, and Jordh, the earth.

TOVAR TERRACE. Pedro de Tovar was sent by Coronado in 1540 to inspect the Hopi villages where he learned of the existence of the Grand Canyon.

TOLTEC POINT. The Toltecs were either an early tribe of Aztecs or a people that preceded them on the Mexican Plateau.

TONTO PLATEAU. Spanish word "fool" applied to Indians of Arizona Plateau, especially to the Apache Mohave.

TOPOCOBA TRAIL. A Havasupai word, "To–po–co–bah," meaning "where-the-water-comes-down."

TRITLE PEAK. Frederick A. Tritle, territorial governor of Arizona.

TAHUTA POINT. Name of an Indian woman.

UKWALLA POINT. Name of an Indian family.

UNKAR CREEK. A Paiute word meaning "red Creek."

UNCLE JIM POINT. Jim Owens, a local pioneer.

VENUS, TEMPLE OF. The Roman goddess of beauty and love.

VESTA, TEMPLE OF. The Roman goddess of the hearth in whose honor the Vestal Virgins kept the symbolic fire burning.

VISHNU TEMPLE. In Hindu mythology, the associate of Brahma and Shiva, who was the redeemer of the universe.

WALAPAI POINT. An Indian tribe in northwestern Arizona, of Yuma stock.

WALHALLA PLATEAU. The great hall of the Scandinavian gods, the warriors' heaven of the Vikings.

WALLACE BUTTE. Alfred Russel Wallace, an English explorer and naturalist and authority on natural selection.

WALTENBURG CANYON. John Waltenburg, a local pioneer.

WATAHOMIGI POINT. Name of an Indian family.

WESCOGAME POINT. Named for an Indian family.

WHEELER POINT. General George M. Wheeler, United States Army, in charge of surveys west of one-hundredth meridian in 1872-1879.

WODO, MOUNT. Named for an Indian family.

WOOLSEY POINT. King S. Woolsey, a noted Arizona pioneer.

WOTAN'S THRONE. The chief deity in German mythology.

YAKI POINT. Probably a version of the name of the Yaquis, the un-conquerable tribe of northwestern Mexico.

YAVAPAI POINT. These Indians are commonly known as Apache Mohave, formerly roaming central Arizona.

YUMA POINT. Great family of Indians of several tribes in lower Colorado region. They called themselves Kwishana.

YUMTHESKA POINT. Named for an Indian family.

ZOROASTER TEMPLE. Founder of the ancient religion now represented by the Ghebers and Parsis of Persia and India.

ZUNI POINT. The Zuni pueblo south of Gallup, New Mexico is still active today.

INDEX

194